FEATURES

WINTER 2022 • NUMBER 30

T0169580

DEPARTMENTS

WEB EXCLUSIVES

Read these articles at
plough.com/web30.

PLOUGH.COM

EDITOR: Peter Mommsen
SENIOR EDITORS: Maureen Swinger, Sam Hine, Susannah Black
EDITOR-AT-LARGE: Caitrin Keiper
MANAGING EDITORS: Maria Hine, Dori Moody
BOOKS AND CULTURE EDITOR: Joy Marie Clarkson
POETRY EDITOR: A. M. Juster
DESIGNERS: Rosalind Stevenson, Miriam Burleson
CREATIVE DIRECTOR: Clare Stober
COPY EDITORS: Wilma Mommsen, Priscilla Jensen
FACT CHECKER: Suzanne Quinta
MARKETING DIRECTOR: Trevor Wiser
UK EDITION: Ian Barth
CONTRIBUTING EDITORS: Leah Libresco Sargeant,
Brandon McGinley, Jake Meador
FOUNDING EDITOR: Eberhard Arnold (1883–1935)

Plough Quarterly No. 30: Made Perfect: Ability and Disability
Published by Plough Publishing House, ISBN 978-1-63608-049-9
Copyright © 2022 by Plough Publishing House. All rights reserved.

EDITORIAL OFFICE
151 Bowne Drive
Walden, NY 12586
T: 845.572.3455
info@plough.com

SUBSCRIBER SERVICES
PO Box 8542
Big Sandy, TX 75755
T: 800.521.8011
subscriptions@plough.com

United Kingdom
Brightling Road
Robertsbridge
TN32 5DR
T: +44(0)1580.883.344

Australia
4188 Gwydir Highway
Elsmore, NSW
2360 Australia
T: +61(0)2.6723.2213

Plough Quarterly (ISSN 2372-2584) is published quarterly by
Plough Publishing House, PO Box 398, Walden, NY 12586.
Individual subscription $32 / £24 / €28 per year.
Subscribers outside the United Kingdom and European Union pay in US dollars.
Periodicals postage paid at Walden, NY 12586 and at additional mailing offices.
POSTMASTER: Send address changes to
Plough Quarterly, PO Box 8542, Big Sandy, TX 75755.

Front cover: Photograph by dtatiana. Used by permission.
Inside front cover: Deidre Scherer, *Child and Mother*. Used by permission.
Back cover: Kim Kichang, *Baby Jesus' Flight to Egypt*, 76 x 63 cm, painting on silk.
Used by permission from Woonbo Foundation of Culture.

ABOUT THE COVER:
The cover photograph for this
issue shows a conversation
without words, conducted in the
language of love. Regardless of
differences, each person shares
this ability to give and receive
love – a bond, at once human
and divine, that connects every
soul on earth.

FORUM ≈
LETTERS FROM READERS

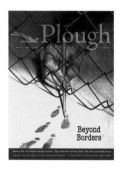

This Forum features responses to *Plough's* Autumn 2021 issue, "Beyond Borders." (For a fuller conversation, see the digital version at *Plough.com/Forum29.*) Send contributions to *letters@plough.com*, with your name and town or city. Contributions may be edited for length and clarity, and may be published in any medium.

A COMMON LANGUAGE

On Peter Mommsen's "On Not Knowing Esperanto":

Esperanto was and is a noble idea. I found it useful when visiting other countries and staying in an Esperantist's home. China had a vigorous Esperanto school program, as did many other nations. I was on a committee touring Canada about bilingualism. We recommended Esperanto as a common second language. It seems to me that when we identify with some culture, ideology, or nation, inevitable separations occur and we lose the chance to be nobody in particular, just a human being with the world as our community.

Jim Deacove
Perth, Ontario

Esperanto and other such artificial schemes to create universal brotherhood may not succeed in their goals. However, I feel obliged to put in a word of thanks for Esperanto. My father, Josef Ben-Eliezer, a Holocaust survivor and an avowed atheist in his younger years, came across the community movement behind *Plough* through an advertisement in an Esperanto paper in the 1950s. As a seeker after a life of brotherhood (and by the way, also always an admirer of Gustav Landauer), he was able to correspond in Esperanto with an English-speaking member of that community, without knowing any English. He later came to visit the community and there, to his own great amazement, experienced that it is through faith in Jesus that true brotherhood is possible.

Channah Page
Robertsbridge, England

BACK TO THE CHURCH

On Russell Moore's "Integrity and the Future of the Church":

The integrity of Jesus got him driven out of a sanctuary and down a cliff after his first sermon. Jesus embodied truth because his life was fully integrated – there was no distance between his life and his words. Those in power recognized the threat Jesus posed. Here was a person of such impenetrable integrity, whose words, life, and being were so unified that no carrot or stick could corrupt him into complicity or silence. I have hope that one day "the church" will realize the importance of mercy, integrity, and credibility. If not, God can tear down the stones and build another one.

Al Owski
Commerce Township, Michigan

By the grace of God, the church is more than its people. Otherwise, it would be left even more fragmented and frayed at the edges, somehow, than it already is. But how can those who long to be faithfully "in the world but not of it" continue to cleave to an evangelical culture now often (though not always) so radically antithetical to the gospel in fundamental ways? What do we do with the in-betweeners, the pseudo-exvangelicals who simply stop claiming membership anywhere because they see so little of the Christ they longed to imitate themselves – or more to the point, who were hurt too deeply by those who claimed to represent him?

I have floated along these boundaries, swallowed these questions whole for most of my adulthood. After growing up surrounded by multiple generations of genuinely good Southern Baptists, a few terrible experiences left me a little more broken (though no less committed) and a little more curious to see what more there might be of faith beyond the version I'd always known. When I moved into a soup kitchen after college as part of a full-time volunteer program, my family prayed for my soul for all the wrong reasons. They feared that I was getting too interested in "liberal" ideas because I felt safer among books than in church services.

I was one of the lucky Millennials who eventually managed to wander back to the church through Christ himself. Every day, though I often continue to hover close to the edge, I am grateful not to have fallen into the abyss for good. But what happens to those who do? Why do so few in the remnant seem to try to find out? We are waiting.

Casie Dodd
Fort Smith, Arkansas

SPECIAL SECTION: RESPONDING TO THE STORY OF RUSSELL MAROON SHOATZ

Many readers responded to Ashley Lucas's feature story "The End of Rage" on Russell Maroon Shoatz, a former Black Panther incarcerated for forty-nine years in Pennsylvania, including twenty-nine in solitary confinement. Six selected responses appear online as a web exclusive "The Beginning of Understanding," from which the following short excerpts are taken. Read the full versions at *plough.com/shoatzresponses*.

John J. Lennon, contributing editor for *Esquire:* Twenty years ago, I went to prison. . . . Whites usually get sentenced less harshly than Blacks, but I got the max: twenty-eight years to life. When *Plough* asked me to respond to this piece, I had just published a *New York Times* op-ed about clemency. In it, I write about mercy, and wonder who deserves it, and if it can be earned. But in a case like Maroon's, the stakes for forgiveness may be even higher, because I don't think granting him mercy is about his character; it's about the character of people in society. What Maroon did was an affront to society, but the era that he lived in was a blight on American history, one with which we still reckon today. I was moved by his apology. It hangs at the end of the essay, and the writer, smartly, doesn't suggest what should come next. She leaves it for the reader to sort out.

Jetta Grace Martin, coauthor of *Freedom!: The Story of the Black Panther Party:* When a person is locked away for as long as Russell Shoatz, when someone is placed in solitary confinement for a total of almost thirty years, it doesn't just irrevocably change his life. The continued effects are felt by his family, his community, and the society at large. The conditions that shaped Russell Shoatz, that radicalized his thinking and led him toward violence have not dramatically changed. Police brutality still exists. Racism and discrimination still exist. The hope is that the root causes and the root conditions can change.

Dax-Devlon Ross, author of *Letters to My White Male Friends:* Ashley Lucas's generous and winding essay on the life and times of Russell Shoatz reminded me of that chapter in my life. Reminded me that while most of us moved on (and up!) from the movement, some of those who put themselves at greatest risk are still wading through the debris. My question for Lucas is this: Is it possible that the revolutionary worldview and radical actions of the BLA made space for more moderate views and appeals? And if that's true, does that not count as an important, albeit costly, contribution to the freedom cause? Lucas has written an essential meditation on the collateral damage of a cold war that this country waged on radical organizations after the official civil rights movement left center stage. It is only tarnished, in this reader's view, by its need to admonish all forms of violence as equally abhorrent. . . . In a war such as the one Shoatz and others found themselves fighting, against all-powerful state actors who refused to regard their rights, violence was a tactic they felt necessary to keep on the table, and to resort to should it come to that. That was their conclusion.

Randall Kennedy, author of *Say It Loud!: On Race, Law, History, and Culture:* I am glad that I read "The End of Rage" though the experience was, overall, quite punishing. That the administration of criminal law in America is riddled with racism and cruelty is, alas, a cliché. . . . Lucas is obviously sympathetic to Shoatz and feels that he has been victimized by terrible injustices. He has. But he has

Russell Maroon Shoatz with family and friends, 2019

also been a blameworthy victimizer. Two points are pertinent. One is that the oppressed, the despised, the wretched of the earth are, as human beings, wholly susceptible to the vices that ensnare other, socially dominant human beings. Poor Black people can also be cruel, oppressive, selfish, vain, racist, etc. That is why we ought to be attentive to the moral hygiene of everyone wherever they are situated on the social landscape. Second, the need to be more rigorous with our moral evaluations is especially pressing now. There has arisen in some quarters a destructive sentimentality that displays itself in excusal or even justifications of criminality when undertaken by marginalized people. Hence the insistence that deplorable "rioting" is actually laudable "rebellion." . . . Finally, even if one assumes the absolute worst about Russell Shoatz, nothing justifies organized society in punishing him excessively.

Tony Norman, columnist for the *Pittsburgh Post-Gazette:* While reading Ashley Lucas's excellent essay I felt thrust back into that era where cops were a law unto themselves and Black radicals, though in retreat, still constituted a potent political minority in terms of influence. Every Black kid felt like the next Emmett Till while sitting in the back of a Philly police car in 1979. Shoatz's story captures the helplessness and rage people felt when encountering the criminal justice system.

RUSSELL SHOATZ FREED

Anne Sternberg, The Free Maroon Now Coalition: At a hearing on October 25, 2021, five weeks after *Plough* published its profile of Russell Maroon Shoatz, Shoatz's lawyers and doctors presented evidence that the Pennsylvania Department of Corrections was either unable or unwilling to administer sufficient medical care

to their client, who is seventy-eight and has stage 4 cancer. For the first time in years, Shoatz was given an opportunity to speak for himself. As he did in Lucas's article, Shoatz told how humiliation and rage steered many of his early life choices and how he had freed himself of that rage despite decades of continued humiliation. Expressing shock at Shoatz's condition and substandard care, Judge Kai Scott granted "compassionate release" and transfer into hospice care. Shoatz had spent forty-nine years behind bars.

For long-time supporters like me, the joy is bittersweet. We wish Maroon had countless days to feel freedom before he transitions from this life, but we are grateful that he is delivered into the arms of his loving family. Of course, Maroon was not the first or the last prisoner to face this situation. With his liberation, we will continue the work of helping others. ➤

STATEMENT OF OWNERSHIP, MANAGEMENT, AND CIRCULATION (Required by 39 U.S.C. 3685) Title of publication: Plough Quarterly. Publication No: 0001-6584. 3. Date of filing: October 1, 2021. 4. Frequency of issue: Quarterly. 5. Number of issues published annually: 4. 6. Annual subscription price: $32.00. 7. Complete mailing address of known office of publication: Plough Quarterly, P.O. Box 398, Walden, NY 12586. 8. Same. 9. Publisher: Plough Publishing House, same address. Editor: Peter Mommsen, same address. Managing Editor: Sam Hine, same address. 10. Owner: Plough Publishing House, P.O. Box 398, Walden, NY 12586. 11. Known bondholders, mortgages, and other securities: None.12. The purpose, function, and nonprofit status of this organization and the exempt status for federal income tax purposes have not changed during preceding 12 months. 13. Publication Title: Plough Quarterly. 14. Issue date for circulation data below: Autumn 2020–Summer 2021. 15. Extent and nature of circulation: Average No. copies of each issue during preceding 12 months: A. Total number of copies (net press run): 13,125. B.1. Mailed outside-county paid subscriptions: 9,362. B.2. Mailed in-county paid subscriptions: 0. B.3. Paid distribution outside the mails including sales through dealers and carriers, street vendors, counter sales, and other non-USPS paid distribution: 350. B.4. Other classes mailed through the USPS: 0. C. Total paid distribution: 9,712. D.1. Free distribution by mail: Outside-county: 1,186. D.2. In-county: 0. D.3. Other classes mailed through the USPS: 0. Free distribution outside the mail: 256. E. Total free distribution: 1,442. F. Total Distribution: 11,154. G. Copies not distributed: 1,971. H. Total: 13,125. I. Percent paid: 87.07%. Actual No. copies of single issue published nearest to filing date: A.: 13,500. B.1.: 9,034. B.2.: 0. B.3.: 140. B.4.: 0. C.: 9,174. D.1.: 1,118. D.2.: 0. D.3.: 0. D.4.: 59. E.: 1,177. F.: 10,351. G.: 3,149. H.: 13,500. I.: 88.63%. Electronic copy circulation: Average No. copies of each issue during preceding 12 months: A. Total No. Electronic Copies: 126. B. Total paid print copies plus paid electronic copies: 9,838. C. Total print distribution plus paid electronic copies: 11,280. D. Percent paid: 87.22%. Actual No. copies of single issue published nearest to filing date: A.: 82. B.: 9,256. C.: 10,433. D.: 88.72%. 17. Publication of Statement of Ownership: Winter 2022. 18. I certify that the statements made by me above are correct and complete. Sam Hine, Editor, September 16, 2021.

Letter from Brazil

As Brazil's Covid pandemic rages on, a small community of urban farmers serves its neighbors.

Claudio Oliver

Claudio Oliver is a community builder and urban farmer. His community, Casa da Videira (House of the Vine), is a collective of families and singles in Curitiba, Brazil, dedicated to "following the steps of Jesus." At first focusing on serving the poor – homeless individuals and directionless youth – Casa da Videira eventually shifted its attention and location in order to live among the poor. It is now based in downtown Curitiba, where its locally run businesses serve those directly around them. It works in organic gardening, waste management, and fair trade, selling traditional bread and groceries as well as soap made from recycled vegetable oil. The group accepts people of varying commitments and beliefs, but major decisions are made by core members. What follows is taken from a letter by Claudio Oliver from September 2021:

Dear Friends,

I hope that even though Brazil has become an international pariah, you are still receiving some news from here. The past two years have created more space for the resurgence of an old phantom: fascism. Presently, 349 neo-Nazi groups are active in Brazil, as well as 50 KKK cells. Since 2019, 91 percent more guns have been registered, including, last year, more than 170,000 new rifles and automatic weapons.

This comes on top of the loss of almost 600,000 Brazilians to Covid-19, a 13 percent unemployment rate, and the problem of millions without housing; government and corporate corruption; violence against the Indigenous and Black people who are 54 percent of our population; the incredible profits of bankers and financiers while 52 percent of the population is experiencing food insecurity; the growth of the number of billionaires among the elite (forty new ones in the last year according to *Forbes*). Our country is staggering under blows from all sides.

How will our community respond?

The Casa da Videira community. The author is fourth from the right.

Camilla, one of Casa da Videira's core members, packing sourdough bread for delivery

Casa da Videira has not committed itself to finding the "right answer," but we try to give the best response that is possible to the challenges closest to us. First, we joined our city's Food Security Council, where we can influence laws and policies; we started a program that's now donating four tons of food a month; and we are supporting the National Homeless Population Movement with food and projects. We joined demonstrations and protests against the government, for life, and for vaccination – remember that for decades Brazil has been a world leader in vaccination and universal health care. We are giving emotional support to those in the LGBT community who have repeatedly been threatened and had friends murdered by right-wing radicals. We want to continue to show love for those who act and think differently from us.

We are working to join forces with others in a new program called "Gardens of Hope," which will be based in a central area of our city, Curitiba. Our plan is to start a commercial organic garden and a gardening school for homeless people. We're inviting city council members, lawyers, social entrepreneurs, restaurant owners, social organizations, and volunteers to help us build the best program possible. We're presenting this concept to city authorities, but also to other players, and are thinking about how to involve the refugees from Venezuela and Haiti who continue to arrive here.

We have created a fund to help small entrepreneurs, small farmers, and people who were recently homeless to get ahead in life. The "Emancipatory Fund" not only awards money for entrepreneurship but transforms recipients into donors to the next person in need of support.

As a community, we have tried to keep our sense of humor and our peaceful environment, becoming nerdier than ever while stuck at home with our books! At the same time, the work at the garden, the bakery, and the kombucha lab keeps us busy from 6 a.m. to 7 p.m.

We have hired a very poor family; they now work alongside us in our various projects, and an unemployed taxi driver has become our delivery man and assistant twice a week.

I did not want to only share bad news with you, as I have done sometimes. We are trying to keep the light in the middle of this darkness. But it is not an easy time. My father-in-law was lost to Covid last month, my brother-in-law and sister-in-law recovered from it, and some members of our immediate family were in intensive care.

Our group is still small. We are only eleven. Our most important prayer request is: Pray for more laborers for the sowing. We will need more help in the future for the harvesting season that will come.

Sometimes we feel horrified, sometimes we check our plans B, C, and D, depending on the developments of the political turmoil and craziness. But wherever the Lord decides to plant us, we are committed to bear the best fruits possible, in any situation, in any place, knowing our home is set in the future, and our loyalty belongs to our King.

Peace for Korea

The Korean War is still not officially over. According to the Quincy Institute, it's high time to end it.

Jessica J. Lee

In July, I visited the demilitarized zone on the east coast of South Korea. It was my first visit as a researcher at the Quincy Institute (QI), a transpartisan Washington think tank dedicated to advancing military restraint and international engagement. I first visited the DMZ in 2009 with a congressional delegation. But this time more than any other I grappled with what it means for the Korean War to technically continue to this day.

I've struggled with this question quite a bit during the past year and a half at QI. While many Americans think of the Korean War as history, it is very much

alive and shapes the lived experience of the Korean people.

I was born in South Korea, and grew up hearing stories about how the war changed the lives of the Korean people for generations. My parents, both of whom were born around the start of the war in 1950, recalled the chaos that uprooted their lives. My father would talk about being so poor that he wore pants made from rice sacks. My mother often spoke about the traumatizing experience of losing land to the South Korean government because her family's home was near what became the demilitarized zone. She struggled to finish high school while taking care of four siblings with her mother while her father succumbed to alcoholism.

The Korean War continues to have a profound impact on Koreans on both sides of the 38th parallel. They view each other with a near permanent hostility, hardened over the years by occasional skirmishes resulting in military and civilian deaths. Former president and Nobel Peace Prize recipient Kim Dae-jung faced harsh criticism for advocating better relations with North Korea, and current South Korean President Moon Jae-in has been accused of being a communist and a spy for promoting inter-Korean cooperation. Formally ending the Korean War is better than the protracted status quo as a means of making renewed conflict less likely and protecting US interests in the region.

That the war has never ended means living in a constant state of not knowing. Not only are there divided families in North and South Korea, for whom there have been twenty-one reunions, there are also Korean American divided families with direct family members unreachable in North Korea. I have personally met several Korean American divided families, and educated members of Congress about the issue. While public awareness of this humanitarian issue appears to be growing, it is likely going to take a dramatic change in US-North Korea relations for these and other legacy issues of the Korean War to be fully addressed.

In some ways, being Korean American has been an advantage in studying US-Korean-peninsula issues. I recognize the sense of grief and division when I visit the DMZ because I grew up seeing it in my parents' eyes. I also understand as a Christian that to whom much is given, much is expected. I want to apply these historical and cultural understandings to build bridges between our nations so that a more sensible, less militaristic path can be found.

Working on Korean-peninsula issues can be vexing. Yet it is also something that grounds me and provides a sense of purpose. I hope that more Americans who work on US foreign policy will consider what it means to live in a near-constant state of war.

Poet in This Issue

Born in Snyder, west Texas, and raised as a Southern Baptist, Christian Wiman once described his upbringing as having been "saturated with religion."

However, during his years in college and for decades after, the religion of his childhood faded to near nonexistence. He taught at Stanford University, Northwestern University, and Lynchburg College, and eventually became the editor of *Poetry* magazine, where he served from 2003 to 2013. On his thirty-ninth birthday, Wiman was diagnosed with a rare and incurable cancer. This led to a renewal of faith of sorts, about which Wiman said, "I was just finally able to assent to the faith that had long been latent within me." Wiman's more recent work reflects the spiritual change within him. He currently teaches at Yale Divinity School and the Institute of Sacred Music, and resides in New Haven, Connecticut, with his wife and twin daughters. See his poems on pages 57, 63, and 97. ➤

A section of the DMZ fence separating North and South Korea

Jessica J. Lee is a Senior Research Fellow in the East Asia Program at the Quincy Institute. Her research interests include US foreign policy toward the Indo-Pacific region, with an emphasis on alliances and North Korea.

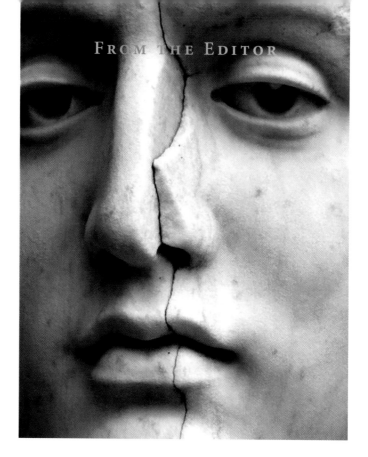

Made Perfect

Whose lives count as fully human? The answer matters for everyone, disabled or not.

PETER MOMMSEN

N SAN FRANCISCO, CALIFORNIA, in July 1867, Martin Oates, a Civil War veteran, became the first person to be arrested under a new city law banning people with obvious disabilities from appearing in public. Passed earlier that month, Order No. 783 made it an offense for "any person who is diseased, maimed, mutilated or deformed in any way, so as to be an unsightly or disgusting object, to expose himself to public view." Oates had been paralyzed while fighting for the Union, becoming "a perfect wreck" and "half-demented," according to the *San Francisco Call.* Despite his military service, Oates was jailed until he could be institutionalized in the young city's almshouse, which was still under construction.

San Francisco had enacted the new law after several years of complaints about an influx of poor newcomers: Chinese laborers, Italian immigrants, and Civil War amputees. As the *Weekly Mercury* editorialized, "San Francisco seems destined to become a 'city of refuge' for all the lazzaroni of the Pacific Coast. As one treads our streets, the eye is shocked at the frequent appearance of maimed creatures, whose audacity is only paralleled by the hideousness of their deformities. . . . Until the Almshouse is completed, some refuge should be found for these deformed 'objects of horror.'"

"Ugly laws," as they would later be dubbed by disability activists, soon became popular in cities across the United States, just one prong of a broader push for so-called public hygiene. As Susan Marie Schweik recounts in *The Ugly Laws* (2009), US authorities sought to cleanse public spaces of people judged to be subhuman in one way or another. These laws went hand in hand with the racial segregation of public facilities, mandatory institutionalization for the physically impaired or mentally ill, immigration bans for the "unfit," and the eugenics movement. In the words of the US Supreme Court's 1927 opinion in *Buck v. Bell,* which upheld compulsory sterilization for those with "hereditary defects": "It is better for all the world, if instead of waiting to execute degenerate offspring for crime, or to let them starve for their imbecility, society can prevent those who are manifestly unfit from continuing their kind."

The last city to repeal its ugly law, Chicago, only did so in 1974, the same year as the last ugly-law prosecution – of a homeless man in Omaha accused of having "marks and scars on his body." Meanwhile, *Buck v. Bell* has never been overturned. While some sensibilities may have changed, the idea remains in many corners of society that those with disabilities don't fully belong. That perhaps they shouldn't count as genuinely human at all.

THERE'S A QUOTE by Socrates that shows up on the walls of the kind of gym that nerdy guys work out in: "No one has a right to be an amateur in physical training. It is a shame for a man to grow old without seeing the strength and beauty of which his body is capable." The quote is genuine, taken from a dialogue by Xenophon in which Socrates takes a young man, Epigenes, to task for letting his body go flabby. It memorably expresses the ancient Greek ideal that physical wholeness is connected to moral wholeness – the virtuous citizen was called *kalos k'agathos,* "beautiful and good."

It's a noble ideal in a very limited way. And in its bad forms it has all too often turned deadly, casting those who do not measure up as incomplete *Untermenschen*. In the pre-Christian era, those with disabilities might be exposed as infants; in modern times, they have been targeted by eugenics, most infamously the Third Reich's Aktion T4 euthanasia campaign, under which as many as 300,000 people deemed "life unworthy of life" were killed.

Much has changed since then, thanks to the tenacious advocacy of the disability rights movement. Yesteryear's hellish institutions have given way to customized educational programs and assisted living centers. Public spaces have been reconfigured to improve access. Therapies and medical technology have advanced rapidly in sophistication and effectiveness. Protections for people with disabilities have been enshrined in many countries' antidiscrimination laws and in a 2007 United Nations convention.

But these victories, impressive as they are, mask other realities – patterns of action and omission that collide awkwardly with our society's avowals of equality in ways that few care to consider for long. Take for example two practices that have proliferated around the world since the turn of the millennium in discordant synchrony with the spread of disability rights legislation: prenatal testing and so-called assisted dying.

Four years ago, Iceland made headlines for having "eradicated" Down syndrome, as one expert put it. In reality, of course, Iceland is eradicating not a syndrome, but the unborn children who have it. The country offers universal prenatal screening for chromosomal aberrations; almost all women who receive a positive test result choose abortion. Today, only one or two babies with Down syndrome are born in Iceland in an average year, usually because of false negatives. The numbers from other countries tell a similar story: a 67 percent Down syndrome termination rate for the United States, 90 percent for the United Kingdom, 98 percent for Denmark.

When my wife and I were nervous parents expecting our first child in Germany, our midwife told us that the baby was due for the Down syndrome test. (Unlike most newspapers' style guides, midwives tend to speak of "babies" rather than "fetuses.") Somewhat obtusely, we asked her what modern medicine could offer if the test came back positive. Her eyes teared up when spelling out the obvious; it turned out that she was a devout Catholic, but was obligated to get us to sign a waiver if we turned down the test. We did.

Prenatal chromosomal screening seems humane – what could be more caring than checking whether your unborn baby is healthy? Except that in this case there is no cure, just an invitation to end your child's life. Whole medical systems have been methodically set up to enable you to do so.

Why would loving parents, who in some cases desperately want a child, choose to abort a baby likely to have a disability? Many say they want to spare their child a life of suffering. Yet as disability activists point out, this reflects a false assumption that may largely result from misleading framing by doctors: as a group, people with disabilities, even profound disabilities, report a generally high quality of life.

Another reason is economic: parents conclude that they can't afford a child with disabilities, or that the demands of their jobs don't leave them the time to give the extra care required. These pressures can be real, certainly for working-class parents in countries like the United States without much of a social safety net; such parents' decisions to terminate may well be made under duress. It's a poignant illustration of the central insight of the "social model of disability": that lack of ability due to an impairment is caused less by the impairment itself than by the social and economic barriers that determine what kind of lives people with disabilities (and their families) can and cannot live.

Yet money is not the whole of it, as indicated by the high rates of Down syndrome abortion in Nordic countries with generous healthcare and welfare systems. In fact, socialized healthcare can even work against people with disabilities, who in such a system are easily regarded as outsize burdens on the public purse.

This is not just a theoretical fear. Public health providers around the world already now promote prenatal screening as a way to save money thanks to its success at nudging parents to abort children who would otherwise require expensive care. Behind the wonkish cost-benefit analyses lurks the same impulse that inspired 1930s Germany's propaganda against "useless eaters." Which serves as a reminder that eugenic policy has usually sought not only to prevent the "unfit" from being born, but also to hasten their deaths.

IN 2002, Belgium legalized euthanasia, the second modern country to do so (after the Netherlands). The Belgian law's text limits euthanasia to the cases of people with "a medically futile condition of constant and unbearable physical or mental suffering." It wasn't long, however, before disability itself had become qualification enough, even absent a terminal diagnosis or physical pain. In 2013, twin forty-five-year-old brothers who were deaf chose medically assisted suicide after a glaucoma diagnosis indicated that they would become blind as well. In 2015, a thirty-eight-year-old with autism requested and received euthanasia after she broke up with her boyfriend. A 2020 report noted that in that year, fifty-seven assisted-dying deaths were of people with psychiatric disorders, and another forty-eight were of people with cognitive disorders; of the last group, forty-three did not have a terminal condition.

Proponents of modern euthanasia emphasize that it is voluntary, an expression of the individual's freedom of self-determination, in contrast to the involuntary eugenics of past eras. Yet in practice the line between the two is far from clear-cut. Belgium, to stick with that example, has expanded its laws to allow euthanasia for children, including those with disabilities, as well as for adults incapable of giving consent (the term is "non-voluntary euthanasia").

During the height of the first Covid wave in early 2020, when ventilators were in short supply, health authorities raced to develop criteria for which lives to prioritize. Some US states listed disability itself – not likelihood of survival – as a reason to deny care. As the writer Alice Wong asked in a *Vox* article at the time: "I'm disabled and need a ventilator to live. Am I expendable during this pandemic?" She went on to question the assumptions behind the pandemic care guidelines:

> Even the notion of "quality of life" as a measurable standard is based on assumptions that a "good" healthy life is one without disability, pain, and suffering. I live with all three intimately and I feel more vital than ever at this point in time, because of my experiences and relationships. Vulnerable "high-risk" people are some of the strongest, most interdependent, and most resilient people around.

In the writing of disability activists, one name repeatedly surfaces as a representative of the view that such lives have less worth: the philosopher Peter Singer, whose 1979 book *Practical Ethics* argues that the value of a life is not based on whether it is human, but on the degree to which an individual possesses self-consciousness, rationality, and autonomy. Following this logic, Singer concludes that the parents of babies with severe disabilities should be able to end their child's life not just before birth, but also afterward. Forty years of critique

"The notion of 'quality of life' is based on assumptions that a 'good' healthy life is one without disability, pain, and suffering. I live with all three intimately and I feel more vital than ever."

Alice Wong

by disability advocates have not budged Singer's position. As Katie Booth commented after interviewing him in 2018:

> His arguments are built intricately and beautifully, like a perfect mathematics equation, but at their core beats a single assertion, one that is still too difficult to concede: that this group of human beings aren't really *people*.

Many others, however, do concede this assertion, even if only tacitly; that, at least, is what widespread support for euthanasia and abortion in cases of disability strongly suggests. Millions who have likely never heard of Peter Singer – who might well recoil from his defense of infanticide, who may even consider themselves disability-rights allies – nonetheless agree with the core of his claim about which lives, when push comes to shove, ought to count.

What explodes this claim, and this whole way of thinking, is the existence of people like my late friend Duane.

DUANE WAS TWENTY-ONE when I got to know him well, four years younger than me. Since he never learned to speak, and generally didn't seem to understand words spoken to him, he likely wasn't "self-conscious" or "rational" by Singer's definitions. He certainly wasn't autonomous: he couldn't walk except for a few minutes at a time in a complex  gait trainer that supported his back and knees, and he required a caregiver to assist him with eating, showering, toileting, and just about everything else.

For a while I was that caregiver. The opportunity came to me through a pastor in the Bruderhof, who suggested I give it a try at a time when I felt that much in my life as a community member had gone off course. Duane was then living with his parents, Jeremy and Mengia; their other kids had recently grown up and left the house. I moved in, and under the supervision of Duane's doctor and a nurse, started looking after him 24/7.

I'd never interacted with someone like Duane before. Like the people who wrote the ugly laws, I'd avoided people who looked like him. In reality, he was a handsome fellow with a radiant personality, as I'd realize in time, but what I saw at first was the contorted limbs, the painfully tight tendons, the often vacant expression, the uncontrolled movements resulting from brain damage caused by a lifetime of grand mal seizures. I soon learned to wake in the night at the change in his breathing patterns that indicated that another seizure was about to hit. Much of every day he spent in pain.

Duane had no realistic prospect of ever gaining more physical ability. And yet it was an undeniable fact that he was fully a human being. After a few weeks I could read his moods, and there was no doubt he was happy when I showed up and he enjoyed spending time with me. The feeling was mutual. Once I'd learned the basics of his care, we started taking expeditions into the woods using his all-terrain wheelchair. He'd spend the bright afternoons lying on a pile of leaves underneath a sugar maple, often chuckling at the leaves drifting above him across the deep blue fall sky.

Every now and then, at unexpected moments, Duane would catch my eye and fix me with a direct gaze. It was a look that pierced, earnest and disconcerting. Sometimes I thought it was a look of deep sadness; at other times it felt like a challenge from one who could see me as I really was. Or maybe it was just a question: "Who am I? Who are you?" In these moments it seemed as if we were on the verge of communicating, as if, but for just one tiny obstacle, the spark of comprehension was ready to leap between his mind and mine.

I had spent most of my high school and college years imbibing the anxious creed of meritocracy, which not coincidentally elevates the same rationality and autonomy so prized by Singer. "You are the crème de la crème," the college president had told us in freshman orientation, and I'd believed him – which meant believing that the worth of my own life, and other people's lives, depended on achieving at a high level, developing one's full potential, and earning socially valuable credentials.

Now here was a guy roughly my own age for whom none of that made sense – whose life was as truly human as anyone's, and perhaps even more coherent than mine. What's more, though he needed help with care, he didn't need me to meritocratically excel at being a caregiver. As far as I could tell, he was more interested in having a buddy.

When December arrived, we mostly had to stay indoors. Apart from the routines of meals, hygiene, and physical therapy, there was often not much to do other than listen to music. If Duane was feeling high-energy, the playlist was anything with a fat beat, especially drum and bass. But on the days after a seizure, he'd often just sleep, and so quieter music was in order.

On those days, since it was the Advent season, I worked through my Christmas classical collection, and ended up listening several hundred times to one movement from Mozart's *Great Mass in C Minor*. In it, a soprano soloist sings thirteen words from the Credo, in a gentle but soaring melody: *Et incarnatus est* – "He was made flesh." The final phrase is repeated over and over, the words dissolving into long melismas intertwined with oboes and bassoons, as if the music itself is overcome by an awe beyond all speech that this event truly happened: *Et homo factus est* – "and He was made man."

What kind of human being did Christ become when he was made flesh? Not someone, scripture hints, who was valuable by virtue of his physical beauty, credentials, social status, or freedom from dependence and vulnerability. According to Christian tradition, he was rather the man described by the prophet Isaiah: "He hath no form nor comeliness; and when we shall see him, there is no beauty that we should desire him. He is despised and rejected of men, a man of sorrows and acquainted with grief; and we hid as it were our faces from him; he was despised, and we esteemed him not" (53:2–3).

Mozart's eight-minute song is the deepest meditation I know on the mystery of the Incarnation. This mystery is not accessible by the intellect. Though we may repeat the words of the creed, and affirm them as truths we accept, we don't know what we're saying unless we first let go of false conceptions of what being fully human means. Once we do so, we may discover

a vocation that belongs to people disabled and nondisabled alike.

In 1961, the novelist Flannery O'Connor, herself disabled by lupus (see page 112), was invited by Dominican nuns in Atlanta to write an introduction to a memoir of a little girl they

To be human as Christ was human involves pain. It requires vulnerability, an emptying of one's own power, and dependence instead of autonomy.

had cared for. Mary Ann Long would surely have fallen afoul of the ugly laws: she had one eye removed, and a tumor growing in half of her face. O'Connor wrote:

> Most of us have learned to be dispassionate about evil, to look it in the face and find, as often as not, our own grinning reflections with which we do not argue, but good is another matter. Few have stared at that long enough to accept the fact that its face too is grotesque, that in us the good is something under construction. The modes of evil usually receive worthy expression. The modes of good have to be satisfied with a cliché or a smoothing-down to soften their real look. When we look into the face of good, we are liable to see a face like Mary Ann's, full of promise.

Both Mary Ann and Duane show the face of what it is to be fully human, fully beautiful and good. To be human as Christ was human involves pain. It requires vulnerability, an emptying of one's own power, and dependence instead of autonomy. It leads to perfection, but of a different sort than the one Socrates had in mind: "My strength is made perfect in weakness" (2 Cor. 12:9). This perfection is available to every human being. It is full of promise. ➴

Falling Down

*When you're challenged by your body,
you must love as fiercely as you fight.*

MOLLY MCCULLY BROWN

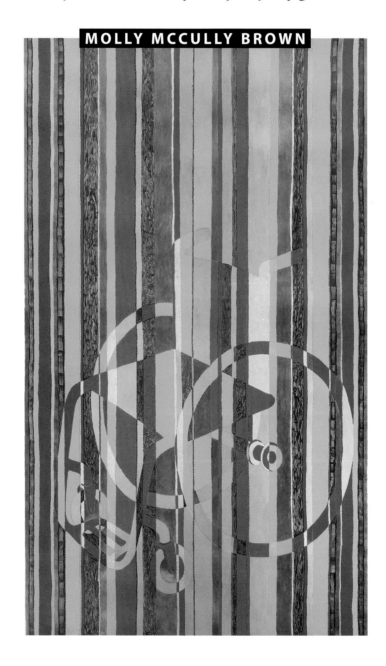

LOST SOMEWHERE in my parents' house in Virginia, there is an old home video of me at four or five years old. I'm at a table in some occupational therapist's office, practicing drawing a circle. I hold the marker in my whole fist and move it like it's made of lead. Gently, my therapist reaches over and tries to put her hand around mine and guide it. Without a word, I shake her off. Then I reach into the basket of markers and take a new one. I look at her, give her the second pen, and move her hands forcefully toward her side of the table, shaking my head. Then I turn back to my own page, my green not-a-circle; I pick up my marker and bear down hard, concentrating. Here the camera starts to shake a little, and somewhere offscreen you can hear my father laughing.

I've been thinking a lot, lately, about the mechanisms by which we become who we are.

For instance, I was born three months early. My brain is damaged; my muscles are spastic; it has always been this way. For instance, in college I decided that I wanted to be the kind of person who drank her coffee black. So I did, cups of the stuff. I choked it down, hating it. Until one day I didn't hate it anymore. This morning I drank my coffee strong and straight in the semidark. It wasn't a performance. For instance, my younger brother has a little extra piece of a chromosome. It doesn't have any obvious effect. It's just a fact in him that might mean something later. And, although I talk to my father several times a week, he always answers the phone, *Are you okay?*, afraid each time my siblings and I call that we're in trouble, that we've been hurt.

I always set my glass down too close to the edge of the table. I have a head for poems but not for equations, or directions, or dates. My earliest whole memory is of lying in a hospital, choosing which flavor anesthetic gas I wanted to breathe while the surgeons put me under: cherry, butterscotch, grape. Or maybe it's my father reading "Those Winter Sundays"; I don't know which comes first. I still can't eat butterscotch; something in it makes me afraid.

I am an identical twin. Or was. (What's the right tense for having the same genetic material as a ghost?) My mother regularly dreams that she has forgotten one of her children somewhere in the woods. Also, she dislikes cilantro and has beautiful, illegible handwriting and

I was born three months early. My brain is damaged; my muscles are spastic; it has always been this way.

no idea how the internet operates. My older sister can pick up any instrument and discern the way it works in minutes, pick out basic chord progressions like she already speaks the language. She runs marathons, pushing her body like a hot, humming engine turning over and over and over. Our little brother adores her. He can name every baseball prospect eligible for the draft this year, and when he's upset, his face sets hard just like our father's, and he doesn't want to talk to you. My father can remember no poems but all the lyrics to "Born to Run." He doesn't go to church but keeps a medal of Saint Lucy hanging in his car to stand guard over his failing eyes.

Which of these things begets another? By what logic do they come into the world? How much shaping of ourselves can we do before we throw up our hands and are carried away by the sea?

Molly McCully Brown is the author of the essay collection *Places I've Taken My Body* (Persea Books, 2020), from which this article is adapted. She is also the coauthor of the poetry collection *In The Field Between Us* (Persea Books, 2020). She teaches at Old Dominion University.

Opposite: Gordon Sasaki, *Aloha Wheelchair,* acrylic on paper

FOR SOMEONE WHO IS so clearly physically fragile, who so frequently can't get along without the help of other people, I am especially bad at being vulnerable. What I mean is, I will roll through the airport in my wheelchair with the strap of my bag in my teeth rather than let someone push me. No, what I mean is, I have a

> I learned early to love that I was fierce. To understand that my willingness to go to battle was a star under which I would thrive.

thousand-watt *I've got it!* smile. No, I'm skirting the whole truth again – what I mean is that almost every person I have ever loved has at some point looked me in the eye and said: *You have to let me in; you have to tell me what you're feeling; you have to ask for help.* Far too often I have let things go to rubble rather than open up.

UNTIL THE YEAR I turn twenty-one, I somehow manage to think my anger is a secret, a small stone only I can feel settled heavy in my throat.

That year, I'm living in Texas and teaching creative writing at an inner-city elementary school several afternoons a week. My kids are in fourth grade, but they do not know the difference between a noun, a verb, and an adjective. Many of them cannot put a sentence together. Most of them don't speak English as a first language. They associate writing with feeling dumb, and from the first day, it's clear to me that they're furious about the hours that we spend together each week. They think they've been dumped with me because they're struggling or because their parents, working long hours, are not free to pick them up when the school day ends. They're not wrong.

They refuse to pick up their pencils. They throw paper airplanes at my head. They steal each other's shoes and leap out of their seats at every available opportunity. They call me *bitch* with a casual venom that stuns me. They slap each other outright. They cry at the slightest provocation, and otherwise they yell. They are all bluster and devastation. Tiny storms. Microbursts.

There are nineteen of them. I'm a year out of college and completely lost, enraged to discover that I muscled through a childhood and adolescence marked by surgical intervention and constant physical therapy in pursuit of some bright and "better" future, only to find myself staring down the barrel of an adulthood that looks just as lonely, complicated, and medically uncertain. My knees and elbows and ankles throb. I resist the urge to yell *Fuck you! I'm angry, too!*

But, amid the chaos, the kids are also hugely imaginative and gregarious and inventive. They stand up on chairs and share all the details of what they ate for lunch or why they hate vanilla pudding. They tell me the dreams they have about space-travel robots and their ideas for the best possible superhero, who would shoot chocolate from his mouth. They want me to call them by the names of '90s pop stars I have no idea how they've ever heard of. For a week, Salvador only answers to J-Lo. Kimani ends every writing prompt we ever do with a list of all the impossibly fancy cars he wants to own: *Bugatti, Lamborghini, Ferrari, Corvette.*

One day, when I stand up briefly at the board to write an example sentence, I trip and fall down. They all rush toward me in a collective wave. Warm little bodies, tiny hands patting my back. *I fall down sometimes, too,* Jerry says matter-of-factly. Like, *Don't worry, you're not the only one.* They nod soberly.

They deserve someone so much better than me. Someone able-bodied. Experienced. Not so busy falling apart. But I'm all they've got for

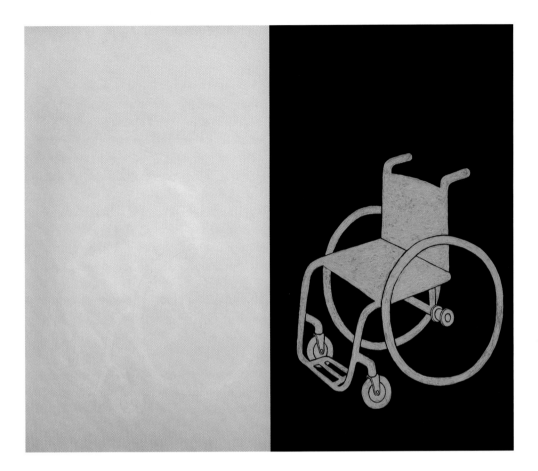

these small hours. I resist the urge to cry, to say *I'm sorry. I'm sorry. I'm so sorry.*

One day, Trevor, when I tell him he has to open his notebook and get to work, looks me straight in the face and begins to stab himself in the chest with his pencil. Hard. I hear the lead break below his clavicle. He blinks tears out of his huge, brass eyes. I have never before felt quite so limited by my wheelchair. I cannot fit between the desks to reach him. I stagger up and trip in the distance between us. Inside me, something seethes. Inside me, some feral animal claws at my rib cage, trapped.

That night I go out to dinner with a friend. Talking about some article I read on the internet about how we process grief, I say: *I mean, if I had to pick a negative emotion to feel – fear, anger, sadness – I'd pick –*

Anger. You'd pick anger.

She cuts me off like she's saying: *I know. Of course you would. Of course.* She means it fondly, but there it is. I'm shocked. I ask if she thinks I am an angry person. She looks at me like I'm a lunatic.

Molly, of course. You're one of the angriest people I know.

She's kind enough to list all the other, better things she thinks I am as well. But down there with it all, she says, there's rage.

I am not keeping my own secrets especially well.

I LEARNED EARLY to love that I was fierce. To understand that my willingness to go to battle was a star under which I would thrive. You need a lot of grit, a little rage to wrestle pain.

Gordon Sasaki, *Invisible Wheelchair*, acrylic on paper

About the artist: Gordon Sasaki, an Asian American artist, has been a wheelchair user since an auto accident that led to his commitment to disability culture and advocacy. Through his artwork, Sasaki says, he seeks to find beauty in adversity.

Gordon Sasaki, *Grey Glitter Wheelchair*, acrylic on paper

into strange cities. And I learned to spin the terror of falling down in the shower, or alone on a rainy street, into something harder-edged that would let me do much more complicated things alone. I am the woman leaping off the high dive, even when it looks like falling.

I feel an enormous amount of loyalty to the little girl in that lost home video. I see how madly she wants her own independent life, how hard she's willing to work for it, how important she already knows it is that she can make it for herself. And so I worked hard to turn her into a woman who won't back down, one who has options available to her and the gumption to go after them. One who knows how to drink whiskey and hold a political debate, wear red lipstick and fight the impulse to hate herself, however flawed and incapable she feels every day. I worked to give her everything I could of the life she wanted, miles farther from home than anybody thought she'd ever go.

Feel fear? Feel sadness? Feel lonely or wounded? If you can turn it into rage, you can use it as fuel. Get mad and you'll get up in the morning.

But somehow I've become a person who speaks sharply to everyone around her. Who wants to scream at children, then break down in tears. Whose rage is always written on her face.

You're one of the angriest people I know.

Anger is part of the engine that makes things happen, but it's savage and dangerous. It also burns things down.

I never meant to turn that girl into a forest fire.

The story goes that I came into the world blue and tiny and sparring for my place in it. Two pounds, with my fists up. *Watch out,* the nurses said. *Watch out, you've got a fighter.*

What comes first: the fierceness or the need to be fierce?

Fighting, I re-learned to walk four times; I clenched my teeth through spasms. I eased dissolving stitches out of the backs of my legs. I bled inside plaster casts and muscled my body

TOWARD THE END of the year, I read my class a version of Rudyard Kipling's story "How The Camel Got His Hump." I have them make construction paper signs with all the animal names and act it out on the rug in the front of the classroom, saying *humph* just like the camel does in the story, hanging their heads in frustration like the dog and the ox. They compete to see who can *humph* louder. They draw pictures of purple polka-dotted camels. I've given up on making them stay seated while we're working. Instead, I say, *One foot has to be touching your desk at all times.* They stretch their ankles as far from their bodies as possible and stick their tongues out at me. I pop a wheelie in my chair and they holler like we're at the X Games.

The next time we meet, I coax them into working on the story of how the wizard got her magic. We go sentence by sentence.

How does the wizard get her powers? *A magic asteroid!*

What is her name? *Alice the Wiz!*

Who is the enemy? *A zombie that wants to get the wizard's power by eating her brain!*

Where is it set? *A mansion!*

Write one important thing about Alice that you might not know if you looked at her? *She just wants to be happy! No, she's afraid of spiders!*

And at the end of class Julie looks up and says, *You tricked us into writing a whole story!*

Yeah! they chorus and nod their heads. They are thrilled.

Every class they ask if I'm mad at them; they ask for jelly beans. Every class they ask if I'm coming back.

NOW, A FEW YEARS LATER, it's early in the morning. I'm twenty-something years old in my apartment in another place I gunned hard for, and I'm trying to put my fists down. I'm weary. I'm the wildest combination of young and old. I don't want fifty more years running on rage.

The thing about the girl in that old home video? She's stubborn, and she's mad as hell, but she's smart about it. She's gentle when she shakes the therapist off. She gives the person trying to help her her own marker to use. And what's written on that girl's face when she turns back to the work of the circle on her page isn't rage, but attention.

The thing about Alice the Wiz? She just wants to be happy.

Love as fiercely as you fight. What an obnoxiously necessary platitude. Some fine thread of devotion has always run through everything I do. It's tiny and shining and down there somewhere, even overgrown by rage. It's the only reason I've ever made anything.

> Some fine thread of devotion has always run through everything I do. It's tiny and shining and down there somewhere, even overgrown by rage.

On my last day in the classroom with my kids in Texas, I ask them to make lists of all the things they love: *mama, Church's Chicken, Bugattis, bunny rabbits, Grand Theft Auto, my sister, being able to whistle, Captain America, the rain when it's summer.* They read them in a crazy loud chorus. I close my eyes and try to hear it.

I don't want to burn things down. But I'm suspicious of resolutions, so I'll just say this: This morning I woke up early, when Mississippi was still cold. I made my coffee and drank it black and remembered that I had made that possible for myself. I watched the sun come up and loved the light and concentrated on feeling happy.

Hey, stubborn little blond-haired girl, we won. We are alive. And now the work is to be gentler with ourselves and with the world. I want such a sweet life for you. I want the fierceness of attention, of the light coming over the hill, of your own hand bringing a cup to your mouth. Of love, which will abide so much longer than the fire. ⤙

SARAH C. WILLIAMS

The Hidden Costs
of Prenatal Screening

Testing for fetal abnormalities is not a neutral practice.
It sends a message.

T HE ULTRASOUND TECHNICIAN put her hand on my arm and said the words every expectant mother hopes she will never hear: "I'm afraid there is something wrong with the baby."

Within an hour it was clear that a skeletal dysplasia would claim my daughter's life either at birth or shortly after. It was also clear that everyone expected me to have a termination.

Hardly anyone in Western culture disputes the wisdom of prenatal screening. It is a practice that most of us take for granted. But what are the long-term effects?

As a social practice, prenatal screening is framed as morally neutral. Scans are voluntary. It is the informed and consenting parents who decide how to act on the basis of the information they receive. At twenty weeks there were only two things I knew about my daughter, both of them scientifically derived facts: her physical abnormality and her biological sex. These facts were discovered simultaneously in a routine scan in which only two questions were asked as if they were of primary importance: Does this child have a healthy body, and is this child male or female?

Prenatal screening relies on society's evaluation of what is acceptably normal. In cases of fetal abnormality, termination is assumed to be both right and necessary for a child whose quality of life might prove suboptimal according to this definition, even though in reality this is a highly subjective determination. Only a tiny minority of parents face the heartache of fetal abnormality. But screening to find out whether or not a child is healthy legitimates the idea of terminating the life of a child whose physical capacities are suboptimal, and this idea affects every one of us. It is reinforced by a legal structure that not only makes this idea plausible but also permissible right up to full term.

In 2021, Heidi Crowter, a twenty-six-year-old woman with Down syndrome, exposed the myth of screening as a neutral practice when she took the UK government to court on the grounds of "downright discrimination." Crowter's case is unambiguous. In the United Kingdom, healthy babies cannot be legally aborted after twenty-four weeks, but no such restriction applies in the case of sick babies. Over 90 percent of parents who discover their child has Down syndrome choose never to see their child alive. The law legitimates an invidious double standard. In an age that prides itself on upholding the rights of people with disabilities, our failure to critique the latent assumptions that lie at the heart of prenatal screening is startling and contradictory.

The practice assumes certain ways of evaluating personhood, defining autonomy, imagining agency, and forming identity. These assumptions purport to be universal when they are in fact subject to political, economic, and cultural forces that vary widely from one society to another. In many non-Western contexts, and in diverse subcultures within Western societies, revealing the sex of the child ahead of time places the unborn at risk of termination on grounds of gender. Pregnant women in these cultures face acute tensions and even dangers when forced to navigate the repercussions of prenatal screening. Yet in spite of this fact, and in the face of growing evidence of the long-term anguish caused by gender stereotyping, we still allow a gendered lens to filter our perception of our children from the outset, even before they are born.

Sarah C. Williams, DPhil (Oxford), is the author of Perfectly Human: Nine Months with Cerian *(Plough, 2018). She and her husband, Paul, raised two other daughters and currently live near Oxford, England, where she works as a research professor and writer.*

In so doing, we become prey to policymakers with a vested interest in ensuring that a limited set of assumptions appear to be universal and morally compelling.

For policymakers the potential of prenatal screening lies in its power to control the overall health of a population in order to better allocate scarce fiscal resources. Never before has the pressure to mitigate the long-term costs of social care been greater. Government-funded screening programs using affordable and physically noninvasive methods, to which citizens voluntarily consent, have remarkable potential to reduce health-care costs by eliminating the weakest members of society before they are born. Social engineers have long coveted the power to reshape at source the character of entire populations – a power to which medical insurance firms are becoming increasingly attuned for their own financial gain. Neither government policymakers nor insurance firms are known for championing human uniqueness, and history suggests that in both instances we should be vigilant. It is precisely because such agendas are tacitly condoned and uncritically accepted in the practices we adopt day by day that they become difficult to challenge and debate.

Prenatal screening practices reflect – but also shape – our perceptions of what it means to be human. By making personhood contingent upon the majority definition of

> Prenatal screening relies on society's evaluation of what is acceptably normal.

normality, these practices undermine the core values on which our civil society depends – the fundamental dignity and equality of all persons. Precious though we believe our children to be, screening encourages us to treat people as if they were commodities over which we retain absolute power of choice. We choose the timing of birth and the number of children we desire; and increasingly, prenatal technologies are opening the way for us to select the gender and the genetic makeup of our children as well. Meanwhile, at a societal level, we are becoming less rather than more able to live with actual difference.

For my family the consequence of prenatal screening was an unbearable choice. When presented with information we never imagined we would face, we were forced to choose. But we discovered that although a termination was presented in the language of choice, it was the only recommended medical option. Hospital budgets were weighted towards fertility technology, not obstetric care for high-risk pregnancies. When I chose to carry my baby to term, the quality of my subsequent care was adversely affected by institutional policies that anticipated a certain parental choice and no other. I encountered a system shaped by a certain kind of expectation.

Prenatal screening is not a neutral practice. It sends a message. Though rarely stated explicitly, this message is powerful and formative. It conditions our expectations and creates a plausibility structure that is increasingly difficult to resist. ⇒

The Baby We Kept

Our son Yusang has Down syndrome. He saved another child's life.

HEONJU LEE

OW DO I DESCRIBE OUR YUSANG? If I brought him to the airport with me to welcome you to South Korea, he'd shout your name while waving five or six multicolored handkerchiefs to tell you – and everyone else coming out of baggage claim and customs – that you're the best. Our son is outgoing, and he makes the people he knows feel doubly special. Each time his oldest sister, Yurim, returns home, Yusang greets her with all of the above plus kisses for both cheeks and a huge hug. Our son is loyal.

He can be really grumpy too. If he'd been planning to play his electronic drums when my wife, Eunyoung, tells him it's time for his evening shower, Yusang refuses to budge. When he was little, I could pick him up and take him where we needed him to go. Now that he's a teenager, we have to find other ways to convince him. Sometimes we can't. Our son is stubborn.

Yusang senses when someone's feeling low and has his own methods for cheering people up. He'll wave his energetic hankie friends in front of your eyes, or blow you a kiss, making a silly face. It might not be your preferred way of coming out of a slump, but you won't be able to resist for long. Before you know it, you burst out laughing. Then he laughs too, knowing he has conquered – a win-win situation.

The author's son, Yusang, and Seoyul

The author, center, with his family

Speed has been our son's greatest pleasure ever since he learned to run, so when he turned six, we got him a scooter. It was Yusang's pride and joy. He scootered up and down all the pedestrian paths and play areas within our block of apartment towers in Pangyo – the thriving modern suburb where we live – rocketing right through games of badminton and baseball. You might think the neighborhood kids would be annoyed, but they put up with his disruptions. Even the ones who have never heard the words "Down syndrome" realized long ago that Yusang warrants their patience. Besides, he's their friend.

One sunny Saturday afternoon when Yusang was eight, he and I headed out as usual – he with his scooter, me with my smartphone. Like always, I found myself a shady spot where Yusang could touch base whenever he rode by. Except this time, after responding to text messages for a while, I suddenly realized that Yusang had not yet whizzed past.

I wasn't worried, but I stood up and started checking all his normal places, certain his orange T-shirt would catch my eye. But, no Yusang. I asked the kids on the playground if they'd seen him. No, they hadn't. Then I made a discovery that set alarm bells jangling in my mind: a well-known scooter, abandoned on the sidewalk.

Our son had just learned to ride a bicycle. The fact that he did not own a bike made no

---

Heonju Lee is director of Malaton, a Christian organization serving people with disabilities in Seongnam, South Korea. His wife, Eunyoung Kim, also contributed to this piece. They live with their family, including two children with special needs, in Pangyo, South Korea.
Yusang's sister, Yurim Lee, the translator, earned a degree in US law in Pohang, South Korea. She works at a law firm based in Seoul.

difference, because our neighbors rarely bother locking theirs; Yusang never had trouble finding one to ride. A bike could take a child downtown in a matter of minutes. It could take him into the path of oncoming traffic on the nearby highway. It could take him – at great speed – down a ramp into one of the basement parking lots that spiral down, down, down below each apartment tower.

At this point I roused the rest of the family, quickly discussing with my wife, our daughter Yurim, and two visitors where each of us would search. Our second daughter, Yubin, had the most important assignment: she stayed home and prayed for Yusang's safety. She has a strong spirit and a brilliant mind, but cerebral palsy locks them inside a body that doesn't do what she wants it to. I wish I could relate her story as well, but I won't keep you in suspense. Yubin prayed.

Forty minutes later, our search had carried us into ever widening circles, further and further from home. We were all fighting panic, trying not to let our imaginations run away with us. I called the police, who began cruising the streets. Eunyoung called apartment security, who announced Yusang's absence over emergency intercom in the surrounding tower blocks, where he is well known. That's how – four hours after his disappearance – our son was finally found. A lady phoned security, saying she could see him playing far below her window. Where he had been when we combed that area, we'll never know, but thank heaven, there he was.

So we have plenty of reason to love Yusang and plenty of reason to feel exasperated with him. But we have one major reason to be incredibly proud of him, and grateful.

The story goes back to a Sunday night in December 2010.

My wife and I had just learned that a couple from our church were wrestling with grief and confusion, so that cold Sunday evening,

I set out to visit them. They were expecting their third child, and initially they'd been overjoyed, but the baby did not seem to be developing normally, and the mother underwent a number of tests over several weeks. Now their doctor had diagnosed a genetic disorder called Trisomy 18. He told the parents that children with this condition are frequently stillborn or die soon after birth. If they do survive, the doctor went on to say, they almost certainly carry multiple physical and mental disabilities. He advised terminating the pregnancy, and they'd agreed to act on his advice.

I knew I had to stand in solidarity with this stricken couple, and I knew I had to speak up for the defenseless child. But in the face of the family's pain, all I could do was pray for guidance as I drove the short distance from our apartment to theirs. I knew my wife was praying too, and by the time I arrived, I felt certain that I should simply share our story.

The three of us sat down, the atmosphere feeling more like a funeral than the lead-up to Christmas. Then the husband told me his wife's abortion had been set for the next day.

Feeling their anguish like my own, I told them that Eunyoung and I had had a similar experience almost exactly five years earlier, in December 2005, when prenatal screening revealed that our unborn child had Down syndrome.

We'd felt devastated. We already had a daughter with cerebral palsy – how could we care for a second child with special needs? Our doctor advised abortion. And with his bleak words about chromosomal abnormality

> I knew I had to stand in solidarity with this stricken couple, and I knew I had to speak up for the defenseless child.

churning through our minds, along with mental images of insurmountable challenges ahead, Eunyoung and I agreed to follow his advice.

We'd convinced ourselves we had the right and freedom to make this choice. Yet as the days went by, I could not escape a sense that a light had gone out. I noticed that Eunyoung, too, seemed deeply disturbed and depressed. It felt like we were stumbling in the dark, unable to see our way ahead.

With misery gnawing my gut, I found myself aching for my parents' support. They live in a distant village, but our hearts are close, so I called my dad. After pouring our situation into the phone, I heard a quick intake of breath that sounded like a sob. But when my father spoke, his words were strong.

"We human beings have to honor our Creator," he declared. "You must allow this child to live."

I was silent. I could not agree with him. Eunyoung and I had made our decision. All I'd wanted was my dad's reassurance.

My father pleaded, he rebuked me, he wept. "My son, we must walk the narrow path God sets before us. Your child must be born!"

As he repeated his earnest message, I began to hear it as God's voice. This father, God, for whom I had been yearning in darkness, desperately wanted to save our baby's life.

Before I could stop myself, I exclaimed, "Yes, father – I will obey, we will do as you say!"

After hanging up, I found Eunyoung, and, looking at the floor, I told her everything. She just listened, without a word. I did not know how to read her silence until I looked into her eyes. Then I knew. She too accepted my father's message. We both felt a great sense of relief, although we still trembled about our future.

Later that evening, in a television program on poverty, we saw an old man shivering in a cramped, dingy attic. "Life is so hard, I eat barely one meal a day," he was saying, tears streaming down his face. A sudden thought struck me: "Those are God's tears."

The next thought awed me. "Perhaps God is sending our child to turn tears of sorrow into gladness." A wave of joy and expectancy surged through me. Even to myself, at the time, my rejoicing made no sense. We already had a severely disabled child – and now another? I cannot explain it, but I believe this flood of joy came from God.

On the scheduled abortion date, Eunyoung and I did not go to the hospital. When we next saw the doctor, some days later, he listened intently to our account. He was quiet, then asked my wife, "What church do you attend?" She told him. "I want to go there too," he said. Since that day, he has been part of our church, eventually becoming a respected leader. In fact, he was known to the husband and wife on whose sofa I'd been sitting for the last hour.

Looking up, I reminded them, "Through whatever life brings, following Jesus is your highest goal. Please, consider everything that he said about children. And please, please, receive your new family member in his spirit. I believe this is God's will for you, as it was for us."

The couple made no promises. The despair in their apartment seemed as heavy when I put on my coat to leave as when I had walked in, and I felt desolate driving home through the snowy night. But in my heart, I vowed to stand by these young parents. I knew some of the hurdles and heartbreak – as well as unique joys and triumphs – that would face them if they decided to welcome the child God was entrusting to them.

That night, and through the following days, Eunyoung and I could only pray for our friends. We did not even dare text them, thinking how difficult it would be – for them and for us – if they had gone ahead with the abortion. Every day we waited for news. It never came. The long week dragged by.

The following Sunday morning, we drove to church as usual. But before we had finished parking, we saw the young husband, running to meet us. "A miracle, we experienced a miracle!" he was calling. When we got out of the car, he was waiting to tell us more.

"After your visit to us last Sunday, my wife and I went for a long walk. We decided to cancel the abortion. My wife did not take the pre-abortion pill she should have taken that night."

"Monday passed, then Tuesday," he went on. "Worry began filling our minds again: What if we made the wrong decision? Then, on Wednesday morning, my phone rang."

He passed his hand over his eyes. "It was our doctor, but he was so agitated, I hardly recognized his voice. He said he'd just received the results from one final test he'd run after scheduling the abortion, and this scan seemed to contradict the earlier ones. It seems impossible, he told me, but the diagnosis might be wrong. He asked us to come to the hospital. On Thursday, and again on Friday, I drove my wife in for further tests. All results confirm: there is nothing wrong with our child."

Eunyoung and I felt overcome. I longed for solitude and quiet to absorb what we had just heard.

A few months later a little girl was born into their family. Her parents named her Seoyul. In Chinese characters, Seo means "to share" and Yul means "God's commandments"; her name implies sharing God's ways with others.

When our friends brought their newborn daughter for the church's blessing, her father confessed before the whole congregation, "Through sending his people – exactly an hour before my wife was to take medication for abortion – God told us to accept this child. Thanks to that, I have become Seoyul's father. God made me her father! Our darling baby is

Top, the author with Yusang; *bottom,* Seoyul

healthy, with none of the problems we had feared. I will tell my children of this miracle, through all the years of my life."

When I got home that night, our playful Yusang was sleeping soundly, oblivious of all that had happened. My heart swelled, and I felt like weeping. Stroking his cheek, I said, "My son, you bear a heavy yoke. But your vulnerability allowed another fragile child to be born. Through your burden, you saved a life!"

Seoyul is growing up. Her parents give us a new photo every year or so. Perhaps in the future she will build her own family, through whom God will write a story that we cannot yet know. But he has taught us so much already. If Yusang had not come into our arms with what people call Down syndrome, Seoyul would not be here on earth. Through these two children, this quiet story of our life – unknown to the world – lights up our Pangyo neighbors and surroundings like a small precious lantern.

We keep Seoyul's photo where we can see it, on hard days and happy days, to remind ourselves, "This is the person who owes her life to our Yusang." ➴

Mary's Song

*My journey with disability taught me to trust a God who
raises up the weak and brings down the mighty.*

VICTORIA REYNOLDS FARMER

*Fra Angelico,
Visitation,
1433–1434*

Hail Mary, full of grace

Though I've only been a confirmed Catholic for a little over a year, I first prayed to the Blessed Virgin Mary not quite thirty years ago, when I was six. I was cast as the Star of Bethlehem in my Baptist church's Christmas musical, and I was nervous because I had my first solo, a few lines about being proud to show the world the holiness of the baby Jesus. When I told my mother this, she comforted me by telling me that lots of people get nervous when they have to do something they have never done before, and that if you are brave and trust God's plan for you, things usually work out in the end. When she told me that, my six-year-old brain immediately turned to Mary, who had been brave and trusted in God's plan when the angel Gabriel came to her and told her she would give birth to Jesus, even though it was scary. So, just before it was time to strap the five-pointed yellow sandwich board over my peak-early-'90s jumpsuit, I prayed: "Please Mary, help me be brave like you so that I can help tell people about Jesus."

Just as my earthly mother had said, everything went fine. I didn't forget any of the words to my song. Decades later, as I look back at that moment, it's with deep affection for my tiny, incredibly earnest self, looking for female spiritual models to follow even then, and more than a little ironic humor at the fact that such a small prayer was the beginning of a long journey.

The Lord is with thee

The older I got, the bigger the crises I faced. Most people experience adolescence as a time of deep insecurity and uncertainty, but for me, as a teenager with spastic diplegic cerebral palsy, I felt the physical changes, bodily awkwardness, and hormonal shifts times a thousand.

I was tired all the time because I balanced physical therapy appointments with school and extracurricular activities, not to mention the effort it took just to get through the day. I struggled getting up and down stairs while changing classes, agonized over the way my body looked carrying books, and felt both grateful and ashamed every time the gym coach told me to run a few laps less than all the other girls. "What if I'm not wearing the right clothes? I'll never be able to dance the way the other kids do. Did that cute boy dance with me because he wanted to, or just because he feels sorry for me?" I wondered at events and parties. These spiraling thoughts sometimes felt overwhelming, and no matter what choice I made, I felt guilty.

Trusted adults advised me to turn to prayer and faith during tough times, so I began reading the Bible more often and keeping a daily prayer journal. The Bible stories that gave me the most calm and comfort were always the ones that offered pictures of women of faith going through adversity – Mary of Bethany's faith after the death of Lazarus, Sarah's belief that she would be blessed as God promised, despite her age, and the bleeding woman in Matthew 9 who had the courage to risk further social ostracism because she believed that Jesus' power was stronger than her stigma. I read these stories over and over, setting them off from the rest of the text in my Teen Study Bible with hearts, stars, and fluorescent highlighters. Though I did not realize it at the time, all three of these stories involve women navigating the relationship between their spiritual faith and their physical bodies. No wonder these were the stories I couldn't stop reflecting on as a young teen navigating a world that felt too narrow – for my huge emotions, for my awkward, uncontrollable body, and for my always-questioning mind.

While this connection waited for me to discover it, I kept coming back to Mary. My favorite story in all of Scripture is in Luke 1, when Mary goes to visit her cousin Elizabeth. Elizabeth is pregnant with the baby who will be known as John the Baptist, and Mary is pregnant with Jesus. "When Elizabeth heard Mary's greeting, the infant leaped in her womb" (Luke 1:41). Elizabeth is so moved by the significance of this moment that "in a loud voice" she utters words I now know as part of the Hail Mary: "Blessed art thou among women, and blessed is the fruit of thy womb." I start and end every day with that prayer. Before I get out of bed each morning, and before I settle in to sleep each night, I pray for a different group of friends, family members, or members of the church body. Focusing my spiritual energy

Victoria Reynolds Farmer works as a community engagement manager for an agricultural market research firm. She lives in a suburb of Atlanta with her husband. She is the cofounder of the Christian Feminist Podcast, and writes on gender, culture, and embodiment.

outward helps me turn away from selfish impulses, and repeating the words of a prayer that bonds me to the generations of believers that have come before, reminding me I am just one in a holy community of many.

When I first became drawn to that passage, I was bowled over by the scriptural exploration of a close relationship between two women. The shared understanding of the women is more implied than spoken, rooted in a shared embodied experience. Mary, who is coming to terms with the dizzying implications of being chosen as the Mother of God, seeks out a female relative who is also in the midst of a miraculous pregnancy. They may be the only two women on Earth who have this experience in common at this moment. Even when we are told of John's in utero response to the holiness of the as-yet-unborn Christ, we are told of it in a way that foregrounds Elizabeth's bodily experience of the moment and validates the common experiences of centuries of pregnant women who follow after her. Having fought for many years to establish a healthy relationship between my spiritual and physical conceptions of myself, I find great comfort in the way this passage grants holiness to that struggle.

> *The power of God is made manifest in his inversions of worldly hierarchies.*

Mary responds in a passage (Luke 1:46-53) often referred to as the Magnificat:

> My soul proclaims the greatness
>   of the Lord,
> my spirit rejoices in God my Savior
> for he has looked with favor on his
>   lowly servant.
> From this day all generations will
>   call me blessed:
> the Almighty has done great things
>   for me,
> and holy is his Name.

After these lines, which straightforwardly express her recognition of the important path God has laid out for her, Mary's Song takes what seems at first to be a bit of a left turn:

> He has mercy on those who fear him
>   in every generation.
> He has shown the strength of his arm,
> he has scattered the proud in their conceit.
> He has cast down the mighty from
>   their thrones,
> and has lifted up the lowly.
> He has filled the hungry with good things,
> and the rich he has sent away empty.

As a teenager who felt like she didn't quite fit in her body, her school, or her world, I was deeply gratified by Mary's assertions that the power of God is made manifest in his inversions of worldly hierarchies. Someone who seemed mostly known for her meek adherence to God's plan reveled in a radical vision of a God who takes care of those the world undervalues, and humbles those that world elevates. This helped me recognize all parts of myself – spiritual and physical – as having been created in the image of God.

Blessed art thou amongst women

Over the next decade, I survived college and graduate school. I got married. I worked at grown-up jobs. I left the denomination in which I was raised and searched for a church that better fit my developing faith. As I passed these milestones, I felt accomplished, but I still sometimes struggled to feel like a real adult. Though I did things that typically delineate adulthood, like get married and get a job, these were often tempered with condescending responses from the people around me. I did not know what to say to people who congratulated me on my engagement, then praised my husband-to-be for being willing to take care of someone like me, or to an interviewer who said

Fra Angelico, *Annunciation*, 1442

I had "done a lot for a handicapped person" and called my accomplishments "inspiring."

As I reflected on these experiences, I felt most at peace when surrounded by female relationships that shared the vulnerability and compassion I recognized in Mary and Elizabeth. Friends like Katie, with whom I shared an office in my graduate program; fifteen years later, she still calls me "officemate." We

got married a year and a day apart from one another, and she is the only person other than my husband and my mother who has never missed wishing me a happy anniversary. She was the first to congratulate me when I finally earned my doctorate, and I cried more during the livestream of her doctoral graduation than I did at my own. I know that she will like all my Facebook posts from a given twenty-four hour

Fra Angelico, *Madonna of Humility*, ca. 1440 (detail)

period every afternoon when her youngest are napping, and that she loves gin drinks because they "taste like Christmas trees." She is the first person I ask to pray for me whenever I'm going through a hard time. I know I can share all my anxieties with her, and that she will never call them silly or tell me I'm making something out of nothing (even and especially when I am). I pray for her, her husband, and each of their four children by name at the same time I pray for my brothers, sister, in-laws, nieces, and nephews. They are *all* my family.

A significant turning point for me happened in 2015 at the "Why Christian?" conference in Minneapolis. I was moved by its mission to contemplate the difficult parts of our faith in the safety of the community provided by fellow believers. Before we all took bread and wine together, Rev. Kerlin Richter gave a Eucharistic sermon that will stick with

me for all of my days. She spoke of being drawn to tables in many churches, feeling moved by the presence of God in sermons and hungry for the miraculous "poetry of the wafer on my tongue." She spoke about how she cut herself as a teenager, seeking relief from soul-deep pain through the locus of pain she could identify. I thought of my own self-harm scars, right where my over-rotating hips connect to my waist. She reflected on how we must sift through negative cultural messages about our physical selves to grasp the importance of our spiritual purpose as Christians. She concluded with this reflection on the incarnate Christ: "I struggled to hear good news about my body until I met the Good News who had a body."

Something within me broke open at those words. That sermon convinced me of the holiness of my disabled body. For the first time I felt free to create space for my whole self – my messy, embodied self – within my spiritual journey. In that moment, so many other things that had given me comfort started to make sense in a different way. The women I was drawn to in the Bible spoke to me not only through their faith, but through the ways their faith was physically embodied. These days, every time I enter a Mass, touch the cool holy water to my forehead, and unify the four quadrants of my body by covering myself with the sign of the cross, I glance down the aisle to the crucifix over the altar, grateful for the Good News with a body who allows me to remember the good news about my own.

Around that same time, I became friends with Emily, who was a student of my husband's at the Christian college where he taught. Emily lives with lupus and chronic pain, and we bonded over our coping mechanisms. Having someone else who understands the ways my disability and its accompanying pains and insecurities affect my daily life is an endless blessing. She is one of the only people in my life who doesn't need extended explanations when I talk about muscle spasms, or the annoyance of rediscovering daily rhythms after a medication switch, or what it means when I'm wearing my pain pants instead of my cute pants. Emily has pain pants too.

Eventually, we began to talk with Emily and her boyfriend Wesley about what it means to navigate inter-abled relationships. It is a very special kind of give-and-take to weather the joys and trials of marriage with someone who doesn't fully understand how you experience the physical world. You develop a deep respect for the vows "in sickness and in health" when those things are in the here and now rather than in some nebulous, aged future. It requires a great deal of communication, as well as an ability to articulate your limits and laugh at your limitations. All marriages require those things, but inter-abled marriages require them in different ways than most. In mine, it

looks like planning vacation itineraries with built-in rest breaks, preparing for high-pain days by stocking the freezer with ready meals, and learning over and over again that I don't have to apologize to my husband when my body and its limits cause us to change plans.

When Emily and Wesley got married, my husband and I were honored to be asked to perform the special readings during their ceremony. When Emily vowed faithfulness "in sickness and in health," she looked straight at me, and I wept as my heart overflowed with the joy of being known and the excitement of a future full of unknown blessings. A year later, we were asked to serve as godparents to their future children, if and when they arrive. When the time comes, I'll do everything I can to teach them that they are valued children of God, body *and* soul.

> *The women I was drawn to in the Bible spoke to me not only through their faith, but through the ways their faith was physically embodied.*

And blessed is the fruit of thy womb, Jesus

In the summer of 2019, my gynecologist recommended that I undergo genetic testing due to high occurrence of colon cancer in my family. The battery of tests showed that I am a carrier for the gene that causes Lynch syndrome, an inherited mutation that impairs the body's natural DNA-repair impulses. This mutation means that my lifetime likelihood of colon cancer is in the 50 percentile range, as is my lifetime likelihood of endometrial cancer. On an uncomfortable loveseat in my doctor's office, nervously clutching a folder of printouts I couldn't really make sense of, I heard her say, "I'm recommending a complete hysterectomy for cancer prevention. If you're planning to have children, you should do it now." For all I know, she conducted the rest of the appointment in Klingon.

That day reawakened years of worry and uncertainty surrounding the possibility of my giving birth. Because of issues with balance and muscle tone stemming from my cerebral palsy, I always knew that it would be difficult for me to go through the physical demands of pregnancy, and that all the crouching and carrying it takes to parent babies and toddlers would likely rule out adoption as well, at least of young children. But knowing that it would be difficult and being confronted with a moment where I finally had to make a decision are two different things. My doctors have said that giving birth would result in months of bed rest and unknown amounts of recovery time. There are adaptive technologies in some cases, but they are mostly for wheelchair-using parents, and as an ambulatory disabled woman, I exist in a strange liminal space. My husband and I talked it over. A lot. Then we talked to our priest. Ultimately, we decided that it would be best to forgo children, and we were given dispensation to listen to medical advice. I accept that was the right decision, but the grief over what I did not choose has been enormous.

When I confessed to my therapist that I sometimes felt pulled underwater by the intensity of my sorrow, she (another adult convert to Catholicism) didn't miss a beat. "What would Mother Mary say to you, dear one?" As soon as she finished the question, I was struck by the words that leapt to mind: "Mother, behold your son. Son, behold your mother." We talked about Jesus presenting Mary and John to one another before the Crucifixion and how powerful it is that Jesus uses familial terms for the relationship he is encouraging. We talked about Mary's description of God in the Magnificat as a God who upends binaries.

She told me that my desire to expend maternal energy was holy and good, and asked me to think of ways I could do that for all the people I loved. That day, the idea for my daily prayer calendar was born, and I made a commitment to supplement it with an additional external action at least once a month. Sometimes that looks like buying gifts for my nieces for no reason. Sometimes it looks like having dinner delivered to a sick friend, or helping an elderly neighbor navigate online Christmas shopping. Staying aware of these opportunities to serve dulls my grief and lets those people know they are loved and seen.

Holy Mary, mother of God, pray for us sinners, now and at the hour of our death

When I tell people I do not plan to have children, they often ask about my distant future. "Who will take care of you when you are old?" "Aren't you scared of not leaving anyone behind after you are gone?" Depending on our relationship, I vacillate between being annoyed and disappointed – annoyed because those questions are deeply personal, and disappointed at the asker's general lack of imagination. When questions like these imply that procreation is the only valid way to impact future generations or maintain relationships with younger people, they do not consider the bonds of friendship or mentorship. They do not leave room for my devotion to my as-yet unborn godchildren, the first of whom is expected in the spring. They miss out on the grace I give and receive in prayer. When Christians (including still, sometimes, myself) employ this narrow mode of thought, it is doubly disappointing, because they – we – do not seem to remember the God that I know: the God who stretches labels, inverts hierarchies, sees strength in what the world calls weakness, and adopts all of us into his family as dearly beloved sons and daughters. ❧

The Art of
Disability
Parenting

MAUREEN SWINGER

Moy Moy

Serin

Sarah

Patrick

Robert

Alan

Sebastian

What's it like to raise a child with
a physical disability? I asked six
mothers around the world. >>

"**J**EAN NEEDS TO GET OUT of the house. Can you get her over for a campfire or something? She needs a good laugh." The text was from Reuel, in the hospital for the fourth time this year with their son Robert. "On it!" I zapped back – no hardship hanging out with my friend. We had the campfire, we had the laughs, but (and I daresay Reuel knew this was going to happen too) we also had some tears traitorously raising the water levels of our gin and tonics.

Sometimes you can't party yourself out of dread and uncertainty. Sometimes you've prayed all the prayers you can think of, and still your child is in fragile condition in the ICU. Robert has cerebral palsy, and he has weathered multiple complications in his seven years. I don't know what that's like, to mother this beautiful boy through every hour of every day. I knew how to sister an amazing brother for thirty-one years longer than the doctors thought he'd be around. But much as I loved my brother, sistering is not mothering.

I think of my own mom, Mengia, who loved Duane so fiercely and proudly, who still gazes at his photo every day ten years after his death with a look that says, "I got to be his mother." She's an honorary grandmother to Rob too, and an advocate for the disability community in our neighborhood. "Of course it's hard," she'll say. "But it's hard in a different way than people might expect. And it's much more wonderful than they can imagine. I'm sorry for people who are scared of suffering. I don't think they will end up knowing how to live."

I asked some other mothers around the world who do know something about how to live: how do they help their children navigate disability in a world that's not always welcoming? Here's what they told me:

Jean, mother of Robert
Montgomery, New York

ROBERT HAS FIERY RED HAIR to match his fighting spirit. He has had to fight all his life for all the things most of us take for granted: breathing, eating, moving, staying warm, and sleeping. Innocent suffering is the hardest thing to see; for a mother it's like a sword in your heart that never goes away. But when he smiles I feel like I'm connected to something deep and beautiful. Physically, he needs help every moment of every day. Spiritually, he gives us the gift of being needed and loved.

It's impossible for outsiders to imagine the daily effort it takes to care for a child with profound disabilities. Sometimes I feel like a Titan; I can take on the world to make it roll for him. Other times I have to give myself a pep talk to get out of bed.

Then there's the toll of constantly having to make decisions that could have a huge effect on his quality of life. It's hard when my

---

Maureen Swinger is a senior editor at Plough. *She lives at the Fox Hill Bruderhof in Walden, New York, with her husband, Jason, and their three children.*

husband and I disagree about a treatment plan, or whether or not he should come to an event. When the child we both love intensely is sick, or needs a medical intervention, tensions run high and little things can set us off. We each handle a crisis so differently and we're both raw and hurting in different ways. But we've also learned to work together and forgive.

Robert grounds us to taking a day at a time – it's the only functional way to survive, and it's also a commandment of Jesus. No matter what else is happening – a world crisis, a personality conflict, a family upheaval – he still needs the same care, and this is surprisingly freeing and rewarding. It hurts when he doesn't respond how I imagine a child would to something kids typically love, like festivals, birthday parties, camping, or Christmas. I'm thankful he has friends who gather round him and celebrate with him in Robert-style.

The best support are those friends who choose to enter our pain and stand by, even though we are faced with problems we can't solve. Often these friends are carrying their own crosses bravely. Sometimes I feel like wearing a sign, "Don't talk to me until you've walked with me." Still, to those who want to help, but don't know what to do or say, something is better than nothing. I'd rather have people say the "wrong" thing because they care than to ignore us for fear of offending.

When Robert was a few months old and I was still in shock, I met Barbara, a mom of an older child with similar challenges. She welcomed me with such warmth and rock-solid faith: "You are setting out on a wonderful journey. Your son's soul will always be free! There will be pain and it will be hard but when other mothers are aching for their children's souls, you will know your son is free."

In his vulnerability, Robert is able to cut through the fluff of our human ideas and agendas. He takes us to the place where there are no answers. He allows those he touches to feel love. We know it is changing the way his siblings see the world. What is success? What are you going to go out and live for?

> Robert takes us to the place where there are no answers. He allows those he touches to feel love.

Berky, mother of Sebastian
Walden, New York

SEBASTIAN IS FUNNY, loving, and caring. He enjoys riding his trike, swimming, and going for car rides. He loves music, and his interpretation of singing! He was born prematurely at twenty-three weeks, weighing one pound. He uses a wheelchair, is blind in one eye, and has a low IQ. He fills my heart with joy.

Before he was born, doctors had told us he may not survive, that we'd be better off aborting. As if he could not have joy in his life. The total opposite is true. We are all the richer. People have sometimes treated us with pity, as if our life must be so much worse than another family's without this challenge. Is it? Our challenge is different, but not worse. Other children can make terrible decisions that hurt their lives or their families. For sixteen years, Sebastian has only given us love.

Jo, mother of Moy Moy
Dehradun, India

MOY MOY IS FROM a remote village in the Himalayas. Her birth mother attempted sterilization after her twelfth baby, but Moy Moy was conceived anyway. Determined to get an abortion, her mother came down to Dehradun – and chose the one obstetrician in the city who doesn't do them. She decided to go through with the pregnancy.

A few months later, coming for a routine prenatal appointment, she went into labor on the bus. The bus pulled over and Moy Moy was born on the side of the road – twelve weeks premature, weighing in at two pounds. Her mother wrapped her up in a shawl and brought her in to the hospital, where a doctor said her sister would adopt the baby. The sister was me. And the baby, miraculously, against all odds, came into our lives and changed everything.

She wasn't meant to be conceived, but she was. She wasn't meant to be born, but she was. She wasn't meant to survive, but she did. She wasn't meant to be our daughter, but she most certainly is.

If I could advise my former self, the bewildered new adoptive mom, I would say this: You don't realize it yet, but Moy Moy's disability is going to be your ticket to a new life, a life you could never have imagined. She's going to introduce you to some of the most amazing people on the planet and you are going

> She wasn't meant to be born, but she was. She wasn't meant to survive, but she did. She wasn't meant to be our daughter, but she most certainly is.

to laugh louder, dream bigger, and care more deeply than you ever thought possible. She is going to teach you about a whole new world beyond ambition and personal striving. She's going to show you a different way to live.

One highly qualified doctor is going to tell you, when Moy Moy is three and you already

know that something is up, that she is perfectly fine and you have nothing to worry about. Another will tell you that she will die by the time she is nine. They may know more than you do about this syndrome or that genetic disorder but you are the world's foremost authority on Moy Moy. No one knows her as well as you do.

That said, you think because you are young and self-reliant that you should handle this all on your own. But you can't and you shouldn't. It's not good for you, it's not good for Moy Moy, and it's not good for anyone else. People are out there just waiting to be asked. Moy Moy is bored with your face being the only one she sees every single moment of her day. The fact is: everyone needs a social life. Everyone needs something to look forward to and everyone likes a little fun.

Look around! Reach out! We think we can't just walk up to a person we don't know and try to make friends. I learned from Moy Moy that we can.

Jeanie, mother of Sarah and Serin
Gangwon-do, South Korea

WHEN SARAH WAS BORN, we had no idea there was anything the matter until she started getting major seizures at nine months. We had tests that showed delayed development. She was my first child, so I didn't know what to look for. I thought, maybe she will get better with therapy. At eighteen months, she spent her mornings at a special needs center, but when I watched her through the window, she didn't have any expression on her face. She sat there and did nothing. I ended up bringing her to the daycare where I worked. Suddenly, she was all over the place, crawling up the stairs to the little attic with the other children, pulling toys around, laughing.

When Sarah was two, our son Sejune was born, and Sarah was so happy for a baby brother. He had no developmental difficulties. Our little family made the big journey to England to join the Bruderhof communities, a step we'd been praying about for a long time.

A year later, our Serin joined the family. With Serin, you could see right away that something was different. Most babies have this kind of bouncing strength, and she didn't. She couldn't suck, and her head was always drooping. It was a big shock for us, and we had

no medical clarity on why this had happened to both our daughters. Both girls thrived in the communal setting, but we still struggled to balance their needs and (for my part) graciously accept the help offered! It's not in my nature, and when a cheerful young woman would show up to lend a hand, it took a new kind

> When a cheerful young woman would show up to lend a hand, it took a new kind of grace for me to say, "Yes, thank you, that would be great," rather than, "No, we're doing just fine."

of grace for me to say, "Yes, thank you, that would be great," rather than, "No, we're doing just fine."

Sarah loved her friends and her school. Even though she had to contend with seizures, and mobility was difficult, she was not really aware of her difference until high school. She met someone on the bus who asked her point blank, "Are you disabled?" That evening, she came home and asked me with equal directness, "Mom, am I disabled?" It broke my heart.

Serin's path is different. She needs more physical care. She can speak a few sentences of three or four words, but they're the ones that matter. "I love you." "You're not happy." (And if you're not happy, you need to go do something about it, or *she's* not happy.)

Now that our children are young adults, our patterns have shifted. Sarah and Serin join in the work and life of the Darvell community in England with their caregivers. My husband Kevin and I, my father-in-law, and our youngest son, Seroo, are living at Baeksan House, a small Bruderhof in Korea, while Sejune moved to London and became a physical therapist.

I've noticed something about our new family dynamic. We're always squabbling! Much as we love each other, we miss our daughters' influence. For their sakes, because of their sensitivity to any tension, it was important that family time was grounded in peace. Whether we got there through singing, prayer, reading, or quiet, we prioritized it.

Now, four opinionated people sit down to dinner, and wow, let the brawls begin!

Hedwig, mother of Patrick
Kent, England

PATRICK HAS A CHEEKY SMILE, a big belly laugh, and the capacity to talk to anyone. In fact, you will not be able to escape a conversation with him; like it or not, he will ask you: "What did you have for breakfast? Did you have any dreams last night? What will you do today?"

Ever since Patrick was born and we found out that he would have lifelong challenges due to a chromosomal condition, I go through times where I feel a sort of tension, a space between guilt and grief that explains the hurt but doesn't put shame anywhere near an innocent child. I don't want to inconvenience anyone, but I feel like that is what we are always doing. We rely on the help of friends, neighbors, medical professionals, teachers; you name it – we seem to always need it. And there is also an intense grief, because Patrick suffers, although he has never cried in pain. Not even when he shattered his ankle. He did groan, but he didn't cry. When he had internal damage to his knees from incorrectly adjusted orthoses, he kept on walking. He could not say, "My knees hurt." He just got angry with everyone. Although he is incredibly verbal, he cannot tell me if he is hungry, thirsty, tired, cold, hot, or in pain. There is a link missing that we have not been able to find.

I feel that somehow because he is mine, because I bore him, his suffering is my fault. Don't tell me: "You shouldn't feel like that. It's not true." Because it's how I feel – not all of the time, but sometimes. Then there is the protective mother lion in me that will stop at nothing to advocate for my child. To make people understand what he needs and to make sure he gets it.

People say things like, "Sure, we'd love to have him over any weekend for an hour," but when you've tentatively asked three times over the course of a year, and it never seems to work, you certainly never want to ask again, and you're mad at yourself for asking, and at them for offering and not meaning it. But there are those who do. Patrick knows where he's welcome! His current caregiver just told us, "This is my dream job!" No one has ever said that to us before.

> Patrick has disrupted our lives in a way we would never have imagined. And the challenge to us is to welcome the disruption.

You don't choose your family, although with selective abortion some people try. I could never do it, and I say that now more than ever; now when Patrick at fourteen is as tall as me and it takes all our strength and ingenuity to figure out how to get him to do what he doesn't want to, from eating a decent breakfast to taking a shower.

Are there happy times? I'll say. Patrick is pretty darn smart and hilariously funny.

He has endless terms of endearment and nicknames for his favorite people. Catching sight of me after a day at school, he announces, "Woman in Love!" in his raspy, half-broken bass bellow, "I love you in my heart!" And I am bestowed a bone-crushing embrace and an enormous wet smack of a kiss.

There are also times that make me marvel at what he understands. Patrick may not have the ability to tell us what's happening within his body, but he has an incredible sensitivity, a sixth sense, for a different communication. There are times when he shows such an empathy for others who suffer, and a lively connection to a very real and living God.

Every year at Easter we have the worst behavior of the whole year from him. He breaks toys, kicks walls, yells, disobeys, snaps his glasses in half. This year on Good Friday we finally realized why. Our church gathered for a service in the nearby cemetery, where three crosses were erected. We read the stories of Christ's torture and death. Patrick sat silently, chewing his nails and grinding his teeth. "Were you there when they crucified my Lord?" we all sang. He had been singing this to himself for days. But as usual, he did not join in when there were others singing.

After the service we had a day off to reflect and take time to think of Jesus and his sacrifice for us. During dinner, Patrick turned to me and said, "Mom, who will go to the cemetery and take Jesus off the cross?"

"Were you there when they crucified my Lord?" Patrick was. For him it's so real it happens now.

Patrick has disrupted our lives in a way we would never have imagined. He keeps doing it over and over again in ways that surprise, elate, exhaust, and exasperate us. And the challenge to us is to welcome the disruption.

Gretchen, mother of Alan
New South Wales, Australia

THANK YOU FOR ASKING ME to tell about Al! You wouldn't believe what an affirming thing it is to see his name in print. To go weeks, sometimes even months without anyone saying anything about him or even speaking his name is very hard. It's been almost two and a half years and it seems like forever since we last saw him, but also like just yesterday that he died. I've tried and tried to think what I could say about him, but I came up short every time. So I ended up writing to him instead:

Dear Al,

As I sat down to write to you, I had the sudden peculiar feeling that you were right here at my elbow, watching what I was doing. I knew instinctively what was coming next. You were going to take my pen

> Perfection does not depend on a perfectly functioning body. Your perfection was a pure soul and an unconquerable spirit. A wicked sense of humor and the gentleness of heaven.

away and tug on my hand till I came along with you for a walk outside or a family joyride. It makes me laugh, it's all so familiar. Unfortunately, it is just memories. And so I am left sitting here with a pen in my hand.

You were the sweetest baby in the whole world. Perfect, although the medical world saw you with very different eyes. They saw anomalies, abnormalities, handicaps, significant cognitive and developmental delays, a seizure disorder, and a life expectancy of months at the most. Pain and suffering were your constant companions. Surgeries and trips to the emergency room. Sleepless nights and seizures. Do you know how often I prayed that I could take away your pain? It broke my heart. I did what I could, staying by your side, loving you through it all.

But perfection does not depend on a perfectly functioning body. Your perfection was a pure soul and an unconquerable spirit. A wicked sense of humor and the gentleness of heaven. Best friend and hero for your younger siblings, someone for them to look up to and try to emulate. You taught us lessons I hope we had time to fully absorb: unconditional love and trust, childlikeness and vulnerability dished out in equal measure with laughter and high spirits. Tears and laughter, Al. These we had an abundance in the twenty-two years of your life. Thank you.

We were privileged to be together with you at the end when you took your final breath and your soul burst free. I have never felt such grief before, or such wonder and thankfulness.

Now you are gone. Or are you? I guess part of you lives on in us, although sometimes you feel very far away, and I miss you so much. I always try to imagine what you are doing now. Hopefully one day I'll find out.

I don't have a tidy way to end this letter to you, Al. It's mostly just a jumble of words trying to express my love. And anyway, you would never have let the pen stay in my hand this long. For you, words were not that important . . . just something to fall back on when all else failed. So I will take the hint, and only say once more how much I love you. You are forever in my heart, in the hearts of our family – your family.

Mom. ➤

When Merit Drives Out Grace

*Meritocracies assume that economic productiveness is
the highest value. That's why they fail.*

AMY JULIA BECKER

WHEN I WAS twenty-eight years old, I gave birth to our first child, our daughter Penny. Penny was diagnosed with Down syndrome in the hospital, and the doctors told us she would have both intellectual and physical disabilities. She would face a litany of health complications. She would need physical, occupational, and speech therapy.

She would be measured on a different growth chart than typical kids, and she would learn on a different timeline. She would, in short, be "delayed" throughout her life.

Much as GDP has become the way to quantify national well-being, timelines have become the modern measure of human development. New parents receive a list of milestones children

---

Amy Julia Becker is a writer and speaker on faith, family, disability, and privilege. She has written four books, and her writing has been published in USA Today, Christianity Today, *the* Washington Post, *and the* New York Times.

are expected to achieve within a standardized time frame. These lists and charts can be helpful – identifying kids with developmental delays offers the prospect of early intervention, which often provides support for families, identifies underlying medical concerns that could impede growth, and opens up possibilities for learning. Still, I experienced both fear and shame when I heard the word "delayed" pronounced over my infant daughter.

I now see that this emotional weight pressed down not because a slower course of development was inherently shameful or scary. Penny was healthy – she came home from the hospital after two days. She ate. She slept. And within a few months, she smiled and gazed up at us with her big sparkling blue eyes. She was happy and learning and growing. Slowly. The anxiety I felt about her developmental pace didn't arise from distress over her well-being. It emerged from my adherence to the warped values of a culture beholden to urgency and accomplishment above all else, the warped values of the meritocracy.

In theory, in a meritocracy, hard work leads to elevated socioeconomic status and stability, and such status and stability is available to all talented hard workers. In recent years, much ink has been spilled over the realization that meritocrats aren't much different from the aristocrats of the past. I, for instance, have always worked hard. I also have White, married, college-educated, financially stable parents. I have both inherited and achieved their same level of education, economic stability, and social standing. In a meritocracy, social advantages can look like the reward of hard work, even if they really are inherited.

Books like William Deresiewicz's *Excellent Sheep* (2014) and Daniel Markovits's *The Meritocracy Trap* (2019) have identified both the ways in which the meritocracy excludes deserving workers and how its values fail to satisfy those within it. The philosopher and Harvard professor Michael Sandel's recent contribution to the discussion, *The Tyranny of Merit* (2020), goes even further in its examination of the injustice of these values and the impossibility of perfecting a meritocratic system of reward. "The problem with meritocracy is not only that the practice falls short of the ideal," Sandel writes, but that "it is doubtful that even a perfect meritocracy would be satisfying, either morally or politically."

These books argue that the system is functionally closed. It cuts off most (not quite all, keeping the myth of mobility alive) of the people who are not already within its demographic fold. Meritocrats are indeed talented hard workers, by and large. And yet what gets them – us – to the top is not hard work. It is birth. Wealth begets wealth. Power, power. Ballet class begets ballet class. Advanced Placement courses beget Advanced Placement courses and SAT prep sessions and summer enrichment and service opportunities.

I now see that many factors other than hard work helped propel my family up the socioeconomic ladder. There were many generations of homeownership. My parents and grandparents all went to college. My parents had stable jobs with two salaries before I was born, and they, like their parents before them, had enough economic stability for my mom to stay home with the kids while we were young. I inherited

On the artwork opposite: *"On World Down Syndrome Day, people around the world are wearing their crazy and mismatched socks to celebrate Down syndrome . . . chromosomes kind of look like socks! Here's a painting of us in our crazy socks celebrating my daughter and Down syndrome."* —Jenn Chemasko

a body type, hair texture, and facial features that our culture deems advantageous. Being White helped me without my knowledge – in getting a bank loan, applying for work, encounters with the police. I always looked back at my family and saw a legacy of Yankee thrift, philanthropy, and service. I didn't see that having access to education, to jobs, to social clubs, and to housing all came at least in part through unspoken factors like my last name and my pale, freckled skin.

> Penny's birth slowed me down, and moving at her pace has often felt like a sacrifice. The reward is being with her.

I could tell a true story of hard work and avoid the equally true story of unearned, unjust favor that propelled the accumulation of capital for our family over hundreds of years. Sure, I could have squandered my opportunities, but that I had them is the point.

A second problem is that the meritocrats aren't happy. The relentless pursuit of achievement and advantage engenders anxiety, which often manifests itself in working harder. We keep working to maintain our status and to ensure our children have what they are supposed to have – piano lessons and tutoring and international travel – only to face despair. Suicide, substance abuse, clinical anxiety, and depression all occur at high levels among the meritocrats. These signals of deep dissatisfaction send a warning that this life of relentless hard work, entertainment, affluence, busyness, restlessness, and achievement does not accomplish much that matters.

In Sandel's view, meritocracies are bound to fail not because they can never live up to their own ideals, but because they rest upon a foundational assumption that GDP defines the common good, that economic productiveness is the highest value for society. Sandel traces the history of meritocratic ideals through Protestantism and western philosophical traditions. In his lengthy discussion of Friedrich Hayek's capitalist philosophy, he comes to a concise conclusion: "[Hayek] does not consider the possibility that the value of a person's contribution to society could be something other than his or her market value." Reducing humans to their earning potential is dehumanizing, and it fails to consider non-monetary contributions that individuals make within their families and communities.

I support economic policies to expand the middle class and open up access to education and employment for people who do not share my inheritance of Whiteness, wealth, and stability. But even if our nation opens the doors of the meritocracy, even if we live into the promise of the American Dream, where exactly will those dreams carry us? The endless accumulation of status, wealth, power, and knowledge hasn't satisfied those at the top of the socioeconomic ladder, and never will.

BY THE TIME Penny was two, we had a whiteboard in the living room. In each marked-off section – PT, OT, speech, and learning – I listed the exercises and prompts assigned by the various therapists who each came for an hour a week, teaching me how to incorporate movements and sounds and stimulation into every aspect of every day. As a result, mornings became a study in guilt. I could never keep up with the list, and trying to pass all that information to the other caregivers in Penny's life – my husband, my mother, the babysitter, the day-care workers at the little school she attended twice a week – felt even more daunting. Eventually I decided to select one essential item from each quadrant. *This week, we are working on sipping from a straw, putting blocks on top of one another, and standing up. All we are focused on is learning the next thing.*

The list became another way to measure Penny's accomplishments. Each developmental milestone was broken down into components, and Penny needed to learn and repeat those steps one at a time. Things that just happened for other kids didn't just happen for her. She had to learn. She had to be taught. With repetition. Slowly.

Caring for any human being requires slowing down. Taking action to love ourselves and others in and through our vulnerable bodies, with our real and daily and often uncomfortable needs, always takes time. Raising a child with Down syndrome or other special needs takes more time. More doctors' appointments. More therapists. More repetition before learning anything new.

My adherence to the values of achievement and advancement placed a sense of urgency on getting Penny to learn, even if the milestones set for her were different than those for typically developing kids. But our economic position also gave me the freedom to stay home with Penny. My husband Peter's employer provided health insurance for our whole family. The state of New Jersey provided the weekly therapy and preschool. I was able to work part-time and also spend a lot of time with our daughter. In the end, our position within the meritocracy opened up possibilities for me to learn a whole different way of being in the world.

We celebrated Penny's fifteenth birthday this year. I know now that the whiteboard with its list was as much my own anxiety as a first-time mother and my acquiescence to an

Jenn Chemasko,
Sweet Baby Hands

achievement-oriented culture as it was great parenting. There are still days when I find myself worried about Penny's achievements, assessing her development in reference to books and charts. And I still find myself resisting what she nevertheless has begun to teach me: a new way of being in time, a way of waiting, of slowing down, a way that privileges place over speed and relationships over productivity.

Penny's birth slowed me down, and moving at her pace has often felt like a sacrifice. But she also has shown me that my fast-paced life is part and parcel of the anxiety-ridden, accomplishment-based ethos that has plagued so many people like me.

At the end of 2019, we traveled as a family to a succession of national parks – Yosemite, Sequoia, Death Valley, Grand Canyon, and Joshua Tree. Penny had worked to prepare herself – we took a mile-long walk after school in the months leading up to our trip, and we hiked every weekend. But the parks brought unfamiliar terrain. Many paths were rocky and uncertain. Our younger two kids could scramble their way ahead, and their bodies only tired if their enthusiasm waned. For Penny, every step felt like a risk. With her low muscle tone, she might trip and fall or lose her

"My baby thinks sunshine and shadows are magic. I think she is magic." — Jenn Chemasko

balance or lose her way. She needed to take it slowly. Some days, the whole family chose to go at her pace so we could stay together. But I also volunteered on occasion to stay with her while the rest of the family moved more quickly.

I might be expected to say here that slowing down offered me an opportunity to experience the beauty of my surroundings, to stop and smell the proverbial roses. But I didn't enjoy better views. Penny and I weren't more likely than her siblings to see an elk. In fact, slowing down meant missing out on some spectacular vistas. Without Penny, I could have seen more, done more, accomplished more.

The reward of slowing down was not a newfound appreciation for the foliage or the rock formations. The reward was being with her.

THE APOSTLE PAUL WROTE two thousand years ago that love is patient. People still quote these words at weddings; the same lofty thoughts can be found on plaques in HomeGoods and posters in Target. But I don't think we realize how deeply countercultural Paul's statement is. We like the sentimental idea of love, but the practice of patience is contrary to what modern life rewards.

Love is patient. Love takes time. Love depends upon slowing down. As theologian John Swinton puts it in his 2016 book *Becoming Friends of Time*, God's way "is a way of being in the fullness of time that is not determined by productivity, success, or linear movements toward personal goals. It is a way of love, a way of the heart."

The meritocracy is built upon busyness and accumulation. It excludes the majority of people, and even those it includes are not satisfied with what they have or who they are. And no wonder – the values of the meritocracy are antithetical to love, to being present and attentive with care for others, no matter the cost.

Penny was diagnosed with a "disability" when she was born, and I still use that word to describe her condition because it is the easiest way to convey the truth that she moves and learns and processes information more slowly than typical kids. And yet the word that seems more appropriate as a descriptor of Penny's experience of the world is "vulnerable." As a baby, her body was more vulnerable to disease and infection than other children's. She is and always will be socially vulnerable – kids or adults could deceive her or take advantage of her easily. But vulnerability is not a flaw in her character or a defect in her humanity. In fact, it is an aspect of her humanity that helps me better understand who I am, who we all are. Achievement and affluence have helped me hide my vulnerability. Slowing down with Penny has helped me embrace vulnerability as essential to who I want to become.

One day I was driving with our son William, and we were talking about how we all need things that other people can offer us.

William was honest. He said, "Mom, I'm not sure what Penny has that I need." William is now a full foot taller than his older sister. He is stronger and faster. He works diligently in school. On the merits of the meritocracy, he, like his mother, needs little. William often helps Penny out. He reaches the popcorn box on the top shelf. He pours the pasta water into the colander. He will even put her hair in a ponytail if she asks.

I told him about how I have received things I need from Penny and how he might find the same to be true. I talked about how I tend to take everything, especially myself, very seriously, and one thing I admire in Penny is her ability to laugh at herself. When this happens, she isn't making fun of herself. She's just enjoying the humor of admitting a mistake instead of beating herself up about it. I talked about how she doesn't get anxious about schoolwork and how she doesn't manipulate other people to get what she wants. How she always remembers if someone has been injured or sick or has a wedding or birth to celebrate. How she prioritizes people over getting things done.

To be clear, Penny has plenty of moral failings, many of which reflect the spirit of our age. She spends hours on her recently acquired iPhone scrolling through Instagram. She rolls her eyes at me when I suggest she turn off YouTube and enjoy the sunshine. She often insists on her own way, especially when it comes to watching a movie. But she does live according to values that aren't considered valuable by the meritocracy. Those values emerge not out of a need for self-advancement, but out of a simple desire to love and be loved. William and I, of all people, need the gifts she brings.

Michael Sandel's critique of the meritocracy is not a religious argument, but he nevertheless sums up the problem of a meritocratic culture in spiritual terms when he writes that "merit tends to drive out grace." And, I would add,

to drive out love. Our culture of consumption and accomplishment is built on self-protection and defensiveness, on buying what we want and selling what we have to in order to prove ourselves. Love is built on the vulnerability of giving and receiving. Much of our busyness, distraction, purchasing, and entertainment protects us from admitting our vulnerability, our dependence. Much of our modern culture protects us from love. But if we are willing to move at a slower pace, if we are willing to shed the trappings of achievement and accumulation, we will find a way of being in the world that is vulnerable and open, willing to receive whatever gifts might come our way, without making demands, without needing to possess or achieve.

For the past few years, I have taken to sitting in silence every morning. Sometimes it is a five-minute practice of letting go of my anxious thoughts about the day ahead. Sometimes I manage twenty minutes. Rarely are these moments blissful. They almost always feel like a conscious struggle to learn how to sit still, how to move slowly, how to relinquish production and receive grace. They feel like an elementary lesson in paying attention, being present, learning patience, an elementary lesson in love. That time of stillness often feels like a fight, but it is a fight that carries into the rest of the day a gentle whisper inviting me to continue to let go and slow down. Those moments translate into conversations with our kids about who they want to be, rather than what they want to do, in ten or twenty years' time. They prompt me to notice the tree outside my window, the moon hanging low in the sky, the warmth of my daughter's hand in mine. They prompt me to pause before I place another order on Amazon. They prompt me to reach out to people who don't have families of their own. They prompt me to give, to share, to love, and to notice again that love is its own reward. ➣

Hide and Seek
with Providence

Suffering from intractable Lyme disease, I look for meaning and fear to find it.

ROSS DOUTHAT

T O SAY I HAD a religious upbringing is an understatement. Between the age of six and seventeen my family migrated through American Christianity, beginning as Episcopalians, passing through Pentecostalist and evangelical phases, and finally ending up as Roman Catholics. It was in every way a more intense and immersive experience, not just a matter of more hours in the pew, than the vast majority of people in my social class or professional peer group.

Every way but one, that is: I didn't have mystical experiences myself. Instead I watched other people have them, remaining more or less impervious to whatever currents were washing through the adults around me. I observed my parents, their friends, and random strangers being overcome with raptures with a cool sort of distance, believing that they were experiencing something real, something that merely psychological theories were inadequate to capture, and envying them that experience without feeling even a hint of anything battering at my defenses, any dove descending on my soul. I found the arguments for belief reasonable, the narrative of the Gospels compelling, the doctrines of Christianity attractive, but when I was asked, in the testimony-obsessed Pentecostalist churches we attended for a while, to *testify to how the Lord Jesus has come into your heart*, I had precious little to say for myself. Indeed, I found our ultimate destination, the Catholic Church, comforting in its absence of such questions, its emphasis on the reliability of the sacraments whatever your inward response, on the corporate rather than purely individual nature of salvation.

So the faith I carried into adulthood was also a pretty abstract and intellectualized thing – exactly the sort of faith that you might expect to bend or even break under the pressure of real suffering, the contrast between the brute reality of pain and my somewhat attenuated idea of God.

And that kind of suffering arrived, to my complete shock and surprise, in my thirty-sixth year, just as we were making a move to what we imagined as our "forever house" – a rural spread in Connecticut, a colonial-era farmhouse with a barn and pastureland and a pool. First, while we were still living in Washington, DC, came a sudden and mysterious descent, a feeling of constant pain and disintegration, with phantom heart attacks, insomnia, liquefied bowels, a burning in my joints. Then, once we had somehow dragged ourselves to our new home, came a diagnosis of Lyme disease, probably acquired from a tick bite during our house inspection, whose symptoms stabilized

The only kind of prayer I could manage was a desperate begging, a hopeless pleading in cool churches and summer heat.

with antibiotic treatment but didn't go away, leaving me cycling through treatments and wave after wave of pain.

Under these conditions – the perpetual press of symptoms, the desperate fixation on finding something to make me feel better – my always half-hearted approach to prayer collapsed completely. The idea of recollecting yourself, of quieting your mind, of seeking a stillness and a silence in which the divine peace might enter in – it all seemed impossible and absurd. The only kind of prayer I could manage was a desperate begging, a hopeless pleading in cool churches and the summer heat, a demand for help repeated endlessly without an answer.

And yet faith itself survived.

ONE OF THE CURIOSITIES of the modern era is the way that the debate about whether a good God would allow human suffering, the eternal question of theodicy, has become a persuasive argument for atheism (or at least against Christianity) at the same time that actual physical suffering has in many ways

---

Ross Douthat is a columnist for the New York Times *and the author of several books, most recently,* The Deep Places: A Memoir of Illness and Discovery *(Convergent Books, 2021), from which this essay is adapted. He lives with his wife and four children in New Haven, Connecticut.*

declined. The world of mass infant mortality, rampaging disease, and endless toothaches had more confidence in God's ultimate beneficence than the world of increasing life expectancy and effective pain-management techniques.

Before sickness took me, I tended to assume this was because in a world with less everyday pain, the experience of suffering felt more outrageous, more unjust, than it did in a world where pain was too ubiquitous to be concealed or filtered out of everyday experience. And I still think there's something to this idea, since entering a permanent-seeming sickness did seem like an impossible outrage to my modern self at first – like some sort of ridiculous bureaucratic mistake.

But what I learned from my illness is that chronic suffering can make belief in a providential God, if you have such a thing going in, feel essential to your survival, no matter how much you may doubt God's goodness when the pain is at its worst. To believe that your suffering is *for* something, that you are being *asked* to bear up under it, that you are being in some sense supervised and tested and possibly chastised in a way that's ultimately for your

I feared the God who had allowed this, and what he might consider allowing next.

good, if you can only make it through the schooling – all this is tremendously helpful to maintaining simple sanity and basic hope. *If God brought you to it, He can bring you through it*, read an aphorism in one of the doctors' offices I frequented: a neat distillation of what I wanted – and, more important, needed – to believe, in order to get up every morning and just try to hold my world together for another shattered-seeming day.

"A crutch for weak-minded people" – that's how the noted philosopher Jesse "the Body" Ventura once described religion. My pre-illness self would have disputed that description, but my sickened self would merely give it a tweak. *Absolutely* religion is a crutch, and it's not only useful for the weak of mind but for anyone dealing with severe weakness. You had better believe that I leaned on my belief in a silent, invisible God more in those miserable months, that miserable summer, than on any hope or notion or idea in any prior portion of my life.

Which is not to say the hope that my suffering had a purpose was entirely comforting when it came to the central thing I wanted – to get better, to be myself again, to shake free of the spell. Because if suffering is interpreted as a refining fire, then there's no guarantee, short of sainthood, that it will swiftly be withdrawn. (And if you examine the lives of the saints, not even or especially then.) In this sense, the real Christian answer to the "problem" of suffering is that we have the problem all wrong, that it's actually more mysterious when good things happen to good people than when bad things do, because if God gave his son to the cross, then a version of the same test is what every Christian should expect.

And if you conspicuously *aren't* virtuous – if you're mediocre at best and maybe even a little smug – and you get a dose of suffering, and you tell yourself that *maybe this will help me grow in virtue* . . . well, maybe it will, but then your reward for that possible growth might not be recovery and health. It might just be another spoonful of the same bitter medicine, or an even stiffer dose.

Such, at least, was my interpretation of the theology of suffering in those days. I feared what it implied, as I feared the God who had allowed this, and what he might consider allowing next.

This meant, in turn, that I also often despised the kindlier forms of providentialism, the talk of God's loving plan and whatnot, to which my savage mind replied, *Great, and what if his plan is for me to lose everything – not just health but money, not just money but my marriage and family? I wouldn't put it past him at this point.*

But I was also looking for a happier narrative arc. I didn't want someone else explaining my suffering to me, any more than I would imagine someone enduring the sharpest grief – the death of a child, the sight of a loved one's body on a slab – would want me weaving their suffering into some pat and sunny story. At the same time, I wasn't at all content with the invocation of mystery that late-modern Christians are taught to offer when the problem of suffering comes up – the idea that it's all just a big unfathomability and all we can do is join our griefs together and lament. For myself I definitely wanted narrative, a sense of the arc of my life in the light of this disaster, the purposes of its Author in imposing this particular plot twist.

When I tried to educate my kids into religious belief, I sometimes told them to think of themselves as living inside a story, with God as the novelist and themselves as characters, inventions of a storyteller who had somehow entered into his own pages and given his creations freedom. ("In eternity this world will be Troy, I believe," muses a character in Marilynne Robinson's *Gilead*, "and all that has passed here will be the epic of the universe, the ballad they sing in the streets.") This Christian idea has secular variations: even people who officially believe that the universe is purposeless and human existence is just one damn thing after another will find themselves enfolding their own experiences of suffering into a larger vision of the pattern of their life, looking for ways that great good came from great evil, discerning a warp and woof even if they find the idea of a weaver impossible to credit.

In my own case, I sometimes felt like the weave was almost visible. There was a pileup of coincidence and strange repetition – the sickness arrived exactly with our third child's conception, there were echoes of family

afflictions on both sides of our family, and of course it felt like my own hubris in plowing all our money into a rural fantasy had met a tiny crawling nemesis. But what kind of story was it? Were we trying to break out of some intergenerational repetition – having a third child after our parents in both cases stopped at two, having a son when my wife's family was all daughters going back two generations? Were we being chastised for our nostalgia, our attempt to chase a different version of our childhoods? Was this just a temporary fire we needed to pass through? Or was it a sign that we needed to entirely change our lives?

Trying to discern the answer was like staring through mottled glass at almost recognizable shapes. There was something there, I was almost certain of it, but I needed some different set of eyes to see what it meant, what was really happening in our story, and what the God who had sentenced us to purgatory expected from us now.

NO CLARIFYING VISION was delivered, and at the end of my second summer of illness I loaded myself up with oral antibiotics, and drove in a stupor with my wife and the kids to Maine, to the mid-coast region where my mother had grown up and my relatives still lived. It was beautiful and awful: Those small towns and coves and islands were the landscape of so much remembered childhood happiness, and to be there again in this state was somehow more intolerable than anything. I walked the beaches of my youth in a daze, as thin again as I had been at seventeen. I watched the sunrise through eye sockets that burned; I heard the seagulls through ears that were always under pressure, as though I were fathoms deep beneath the sea. My children played on the sandbar, my infant son splashed in the saltwater puddles, and my beloved wife

watched me watching them. A veil of pain was drawn between me and everything I loved.

On the last morning, I was up early as always and I carried my son, now six months old and heavy, down the long, low-tide strip of sand. The pain was mostly in one shoulder, though I knew it would be somewhere else soon enough. There was a spot where the sand gave way to barnacled rocks bewigged with seaweed, where the tide met the stones; sometimes in her youth, my mother had found sand dollars there. I had never found one in decades of looking, and over time it had become a game I played – *If I find one today, it means that God exists. If I find one today, it means that the girl I have a crush on has a crush on me. If I find one today, it means I'll get into the college I want. If I find one today, it means . . .*

Inevitably, I had been playing the game all that vacation week, casually glancing in the shallows as I waded with my kids.

If I find one it means I will get better.
If I find one it means I will get better.
If I find one it means I will get better.

On that last day, though, I was in too much pain to play. I held my son in my right arm, watching the seagulls sweep above, feeling the fire spread down my left arm and side. At a certain point, the combination of beauty and agony broke me, and I began to sob there, on the empty sandbar beside the flat, blue bay, while my son cooed curiously, and from somewhere in the depths I came out with a desperate, rasping croak.

"Help me, God. Why won't you help me?"

My eyes dropped to the water. There between my feet, as tiny as a nickel and as pale as a wedding dress, was the only sand dollar I have ever found. ⤙

Eyvind Earle,
Red Leaves

So Trued to a Roar

So trued to a roar,
so accustomed to a grimace
of against, I hardly noticed
it was over.

Like an invalid I crept
out into the open
(since when was there an open?)
and like a revenant lipped

the names of things
turned things again:
white pine, quaking aspen,
shagbark that by all rights

should have been shorn.
Was it for this, I asked
(since when was there someone to ask?)
that I was born?

No answer, unless of leaves
acquiring light, and small lives
going about their business
of being less,

and on the clear pond
(and in the clearer beyond)
the mien of a man
unraptured back to man.

CHRISTIAN WIMAN ➤

The World Turned Right-Side Up

Was Saint Paul's famous "thorn in the flesh" a disability?

ISAAC T. SOON

FOR MOST OF WESTERN HISTORY, at least from the fourth century BC to the thirteenth century AD, philosophers and doctors believed that the phenomenon of "seeing" happened when light came out of our eyes to illuminate the world around us. Plato, in his *Timaeus*, argued that the fire in our eyes combined with the fire of the sun to "touch" objects around us. This incandescent intimacy allows our souls to apprehend the world. From this perspective, a sighted person's visual assessment of another person – the first glance – is also the first time one reaches out and touches the other.

The very first things that people who are sighted notice about those we meet for the first time are the things most readily available to our visual sense. Eye color. Skin color. Height. Weight. Clothing. Our eyes overload our brains with visual data, and before we know it our neurons are intoxicated with information about the other person.

The way women's bodies are presented on billboards and on the feeds of influencers, devoid of blemish and bursting with exaggerated color, testifies to the power of the human gaze. Do you have a mark on your skin? We've got a filter for that. Do you want to look forty years younger? Not a problem. Vibrancy is vivacity, and the eyes never lie. Bodies must be perfected lest, God forbid, the viewer might turn away. And if they turn away, they don't buy anything. They don't follow. They don't press "subscribe."

But whom we should follow is not always as apparent to a first glance as we might hope. The

---

Isaac T. Soon is Assistant Professor of Religious Studies (New Testament) at Crandall University.

eye is a fickle instrument. People, like books, shouldn't be judged by how they appear.

The human ability to measure up the whole of a person in a glance is truly remarkable and terrible. *They're wearing [insert clothing], they must be rich. Their skin is [insert color], I don't feel safe around them. They are [insert weight observation], they must be lazy.*

Judging others by physical appearance is not a recent development. In the ancient Mediterranean world, people from Athens to Rome and Qumran to Asia Minor assessed the characters of other people by aspects of their bodies, by their physiognomies. Aristotle explored the idea in his *Prior Analytics* and commented in the *Generation of Animals* on practitioners who attributed meaning to a resemblance to a calf or a sheep. There were handbooks that cataloged all sorts of physical features and what they signified: Someone with a head of waving tawny hair might be proud as a lion. Someone with a big nose was probably wealthy, literally or in spirit.

Determining the value of other people's bodies, however, was not reserved only for those who consulted physiognomic handbooks. Ancient literature, dinnerware, mosaics, statues, and many other kinds of visual culture all pushed particular bodily ideals. They were a sort of physiognomic propaganda, putting ideal bodies in heroic postures and denigrating the less than perfect as barbaric, animalistic, and laughable. The beautiful was the good. The unbeautiful, the immoral.

Paul the Apostle struggled with the bodily ideals of his own world. His Letter to the Galatians explains why circumcision is not beneficial for non-Jewish believers. His correspondence with the assemblies in Corinth includes consideration of his own weak body.

In Paul's Second Letter to the Corinthians, he responds to members of the congregations who have called his speech "contemptible" and said that his bodily presence is weak (2 Cor. 10:10). In comparison to a group of "super-apostles" (2 Cor. 11:5), Paul lacks the kind of physical finesse and charisma the Corinthians were used to seeing among philosophers and sophists. But rather than explain away his poor speaking skills and weak body, Paul doubles down and instead boasts about the experiences of his suffering in greater detail. He has been stoned by synagogue authorities, beaten by the rods of the Roman fasces, wrecked at sea, left starving and naked and cold and anxious. Even his alleged divinatory and prophetic skills – his ability to ascend into the heavens – are muted and he is unable to reveal divine oracles he has heard in paradise.

In comparison to many bodily ideals of the day, Paul's body appeared weak, diminished, and slavish. As the work of Jennifer Glancy has shown, bodily scars such as those mentioned by Paul in Galatians 6:17 meant different things, depending on how and why they were acquired. A soldier returning from glorious battle with scars and lacerations on the front of his body bore marks of bravery, courage, and honor. Wounds on his back, however, might imply retreat and cowardice. Paul's scars were the marks of beatings: that is, of criminality or enslavement. In the wider pagan world, Paul's "marks of Christ" cast him as servile and an enemy of the state. Suddenly, the caution of the Corinthian congregations makes sense. Why should they trust someone who looked like that?

The details of Paul's battered body were not the only problematic aspects of his physique. The famous "thorn in the flesh" mentioned in 2 Corinthians 12:7–10 has tested the exegetical ingenuity of interpreters for hundreds of years. A head injury, malaria, blindness, depression, even lust – all have been suggested. No single explanation has garnered lasting support.

Inasmuch as there is scholarly agreement

about this, however, that agreement points to the thorn as a literal phenomenon that afflicted Paul's actual body. Tempting as it may be to take his words as metaphorical, the phrase "in the flesh" most likely refers to the location of this thorn: Paul's body is in pain. But that affliction turns out to be a gift from God.

In recent years one of the ways that commentators have spoken of this affliction has been in the language of disability. Although some contemporary implications of the term "disability" are culturally specific, the reality of conditions that depart from ideal bodily forms and functions exists in all cultures.

Three times, Paul petitions God to heal him, to remove the thorn, and three times God says no. How could he refuse? God entrusted his precious gospel to the Gentiles to Paul, and Paul had suffered so much along the way. Surely, "health" and "wholeness" are necessary for him to complete his divine mandate? To Paul's shock, the opposite is true. When he turns to God for healing, he receives no reprieve. It is not as though Paul acts outside of what was common practice at the time. Most people went to temples of healing, seeking gods like Aesculapius to restore their bodies from the ailments that plagued them. Paul goes to the most powerful God he knows – the God of Israel – but no respite from his disability is given.

Rather, God says that his power is perfected in weakness.

From then on Paul's tune changes. He stops asking for "healing" and instead boasts of his "weakness." In 2 Corinthians 12:10, he makes a bold and paradoxical statement: "For when I am weak, then I am strong." This phrase baffles interpreters. In what way is weakness strength? Is it merely a change of perception? A kind of "self-help" mantra, to manifest a good life, a "word of faith" speaking things into being? Or is it a reality, a changing of the very nature of things? Paul may mean a little bit of both.

About the photographer: Joe James took up photography to combat depression after he discovered he was autistic at age thirty-two. As he found, "Photography didn't save me from being autistic, it saved me from my anxiety." Joe now sees his autism as a gift that allows him to view the world through a different lens, and online he goes by the name of "Joe James the Autistic Photographer."

"I love photography, it's my art, my expression, it gives me another type of voice, to show visually how I feel," he explains. "Through my pictures I can show people how I feel because a lot of the time I can't really express myself. Especially over social media. This is how I interpret what I see. This is where I find beauty." See more of his work at *joe-james-photography.picfair.com*.

Paul does not merely trade labels between what is strong and what is weak. He is not simply re-branding his condition. The revelation Paul has is that, though the world understands his disability as weakness, he has come to realize that it is actually powerful. It is not to be done away with, or put to the side, or remedied through physical healing. Paul's disability is essential for the mission that God has set out for him. Not only that, however, but disability more generally is absolutely central to faith in Jesus Christ. Disability is the crux of Paul's gospel message.

In the life and body of the man whose job it was to bring the gospel to the nations, physical disability was a crucial and honorable witness to God's own strength. Paul's life was an inversion of cultural notions that presumed human existence without pain and suffering was the divine ideal. It is instructive to remember, too, that even in Christ's own glorified body, his wounds remain – no longer a source of suffering but a sign of victory.

The paradox of power in weakness finds its significance in the paradox of Jesus' death through crucifixion as life-giving and miraculous (2 Cor. 4). The crucified Messiah is for Paul the symbol of divine victory over the forces of sin and death. For everyone else, Jew and non-Jew, this weakness of the cross was a shame and a scandal. The same goes for Paul's thorn. To the whole world, his disability is a mark against his life and the power of the God he serves. But for Paul, his disability is the locus of God's power. It is where God's power is most at work.

Paul's paradox of power in weakness puts disability right where it belongs. Disability isn't at the margins. It's not liminal. It doesn't dwell in the interstitial spaces. It is at the center. It brings everything together. To remove disability from Christ was to remove the scandal of the cross, and while his pagan interlocutors would no doubt have found this paradox to be nonsense – a world turned upside down – for Paul the role of God's power in weakness was a sign that the world had been finally turned right-side up. ⤳

Eyvind Earle,
White Rock

No Omen but Awe

I thought it would all resolve
one day in diamond time.
Life like a gem to lift to the squint
as through a jeweler's loupe.

I thought every facet and flaw
neither facet nor flaw in some final shine;
chance and choice uncanny cognates;
form, fate.

Now I am here.
No diamond, no time, no omen but awe
that a whirlwind could in not cohering cohere.
Loss is my gift, bewilderment my bow.

CHRISTIAN WIMAN

Unfinished Revolution

On the long road toward dignity for people with disabilities, we've gone far – but not nearly far enough.

JOE KEIDERLING

A T THE BEGINNING of World War II, Wilmot Durgin, a twenty-three-year-old graduate of the University of North Carolina, was passed over for conscription because of a perforated eardrum. That changed a year later as the Army cast a wider net. But by that time Durgin knew he could not fight; he wanted no part of the apparatus of war. When he arrived at Fort Bragg he registered his intent to refuse service for reasons of conscience.

At the base, unsurprisingly, he found little understanding for his scruples. He had to wear a giant 4-E – for "conscientious objector" – on his back. But Durgin stubbornly held his ground, and "took part in nothing that would make me be a part of the system." Eventually

Joe Keiderling is general manager of Rifton Equipment and lives at the Bruderhof's Woodcrest community in upstate New York.

he was sent to a Civilian Public Service (CPS) camp where conscientious objectors were assigned to do "work of public importance" as an alternative to military service.

From there he volunteered for service at Maine's Pownal State School. Founded in 1907 for "idiotic and feeble-minded" children,

Wilmot Durgin

Pownal had become, essentially, a warehouse for people with disabilities. What Durgin and his fifteen fellow volunteers found there shocked them: filth, stench, sickness, and pervasive loneliness and despair. Though he and his associates tried to speak up, they were fighting years of institutional inertia. For Durgin the breaking point arrived when a school "escapee" was returned to Pownal and, as public punishment, was injected with a vomit-inducing emetic by the school doctor. Durgin walked off the job in protest, knowing he would be considered AWOL and subject to criminal charges under military law. He moved in with his brother in New Jersey, and wrote to the government, explaining "exactly what I thought about the treatments in [Pownal] and also about my views on conscription. I also told them where I was living and if they wanted me they should come and get me," he later related in a 1997 memoir.

Five months later he was arrested and sentenced to six months in prison. Did his lonely stand have any effect? We don't know. But there are moments that demand change. Sometimes change follows from a horrifying event, but more often transformation is brought about by single acts of moral outrage, sometimes years apart, sometimes with no apparent connection to each other. How the United States moved away from state schools like Pownal to a more humane, inclusive approach to its citizens with disabilities is a story of many disparate acts like Durgin's.

A T THE TIME of Durgin's deployment to Maine, around 3,000 other conscientious objectors had been assigned to dozens of state schools and mental hospitals across the country. This was partly in response to the acute staffing shortage brought on by the war effort; reports of one doctor covering a thousand patients were not unusual. Many of these young men, having already acted once on conscience to oppose a war that most considered good and necessary, were uniquely sensitive to the offensive conditions that they found.

They were also, as a group, better educated than the people most often hired at such institutions and better equipped to gather information and describe what they were seeing. Several organized to found the Mental Hygiene Program, later the National Mental Health Foundation, to advocate for reform. Four volunteers who had been assigned to the Philadelphia State Hospital collected accounts from fellow conscientious objectors around the country, and collaborated with the muckraking journalist Albert Maisel to publish their findings in *Life* magazine. In "Bedlam 1946: U.S. Mental Hospitals Are a Shame and Disgrace," he wrote:

> Beatings and murders are hardly the most significant of the indignities we have heaped upon most of the 600,000 guiltless patient-prisoners of over 180 state mental institutions. We feed thousands a starvation diet. . . . We jam-pack men, women, and sometimes even children into hundred-year-old firetraps in wards so crowded that the floors cannot be seen between the rickety cots, while thousands more sleep on ticks, on blankets, or on the bare floors. . . . Hundreds – of my own knowledge and

sight – spend twenty-four hours a day in stark and filthy nakedness. . . . Thousands spend their days – often for weeks at a stretch – locked in devices euphemistically called "restraints". . . . Hundreds are confined in "lodges" – bare bedless rooms reeking with filth and feces – by day lit only through half-inch holes through steel-plated windows, by night merely black tombs in which the cries of the insane echo unheard from the peeling plaster of the walls.

Maisel's journalism, along with that of Albert Deutsch in *PM*, a New York newspaper, generated an outcry and unprecedented public scrutiny. There were other painfully graphic accounts – as early as 1943, stories arising from the efforts of CPS volunteers started coming out of Cleveland State Hospital. Van Geiger, another CPS volunteer, was so outspoken in protest against the abuses he saw at Virginia's Eastern State Hospital that a formal investigation was launched and gained extensive and sympathetic coverage in the *Richmond Times-Dispatch*.

Reports from conscientious objectors assigned to Hudson River State Hospital in Poughkeepsie, New York, attracted the attention of Eleanor Roosevelt, who wrote about it in her syndicated column "My Day." Mike Gorman, a journalist for the *Daily Oklahoman*, wrote a series of articles on the disgrace at the mental hospitals in his state, starting with "Misery Rules in State Shadowland." In 1946 Mary Jane Ward published *The Snake Pit*, a novel drawing on her own experience as a mental patient in a New York asylum. An Oscar-nominated movie followed, starring Olivia de Havilland, with an accompanying cover story in *Time*. Other books appeared, among them *Out of Sight, Out of Mind*, by Frank L. Wright in 1947, and *The Shame of the States* by Deutsch in 1948.

Rosemary Kennedy ready to be presented at the British Royal Court, 1938

DESPITE THE UPSWELL OF EXPOSURE and protest, no real change came to these institutions until they collided with the story of the Kennedy family.

Rosemary Kennedy was the oldest daughter of Joseph Kennedy – patriarch, millionaire, ambassador, statesman – and his wife Rose. Born in 1918, she grew up in a family of overachievers, athletes, scholars, and competitors. But Rosemary was different. Her mother's home nurse, reluctant to deliver the baby before the arrival of the family doctor, tried to stall the birth. The doctor was delayed for hours, overwhelmed by his patient load as the Spanish flu pandemic swept through Boston. Deprived of oxygen, Rosemary suffered brain damage.

Through her childhood and youth she appeared normal but her behavior was unpredictable and her cognitive development poor. Her father became increasingly anxious about her and what she might do. In desperation he turned to an experimental treatment that was gaining attention at the time, lobotomy, and when Rosemary was twenty-three he had her submitted to this procedure. She was never the same again.

"It would not take long – a few hours at the most – before the surgeons recognized that the surgery had gone horribly awry. Rosemary

would emerge from the lobotomy almost completely disabled," writes Kate Clifford Larson in *Rosemary: The Hidden Kennedy Daughter* (2015).

Rosemary was cared for at a comfortable private facility in Wisconsin run by the Sisters of Saint Francis of Assisi, a far cry from the state hospitals that had elicited public protest in the 1940s. Like other institutionalized, disabled people at the time, she was isolated from the outside world: her many siblings didn't even know her whereabouts for years. But later they – especially her elder brother Jack and her sister Eunice Kennedy Shriver – found inspiration in her for both public and private activism.

While President Kennedy signed the Community Mental Health Act in 1963, Eunice and her husband, Sargent Shriver, pursued philanthropic solutions, supporting organizations devoted to research, medical care, education, and programs such as the Special Olympics. And most importantly, the family started to speak publicly about their sister and what they had learned through her.

In 1965, Robert Kennedy, then the junior senator from New York, paid a visit to the Willowbrook State School on Staten Island, at the time housing 6,200 residents in a space designed for 4,000. At the press conference that followed he called it a "snake pit," directing renewed public attention to a tragic flaw in national help for the needs of people with disabilities.

More and more often such attention was demanded. In 1972, a young reporter named Geraldo Rivera revisited Willowbrook, breaking through the surrounding fence and filming hospital conditions. Rivera said residents were treated like "human vegetables," calling the situation "a disgrace to all of us. This place isn't a school, it's a dark corner where we throw children who aren't pretty to look at. It's the big town's leper colony."

This proved a defining moment in the disability rights movement. There is a straight line from the Willowbrook report to the passage of the landmark Education for All Handicapped Children Act of 1975. Senator Ted Kennedy, the youngest of Rosemary's siblings, was notable among the cosponsors and went on to become a champion in Congress for the rights of the disabled. Over the course of the next fifteen years the law's declaration that every child, regardless of disability, is entitled to a free public education "in the least restrictive environment" helped close the warehousing institutions and inspire innovations that affected thousands of families across the country.

When they finally did shut down in the 1980s and '90s, many of the abandoned institutions were considered haunted. At least one of them, the Pennhurst State School and Hospital, was repurposed as a haunted house, as if the property had not seen enough horror already. Located at an oxbow of the Schuylkill River in southeastern Pennsylvania, Pennhurst opened in 1903 and was plagued with stories of abuse and abysmal neglect until it finally closed in 1987 (ten years after a judge's ruling to shut it down). Today, tourists with a fascination for the occult can pay for guided tours, haunted thrills, and even paranormal "investigations." If nothing else, it serves as a painful reminder of how poorly we cared for our own most vulnerable citizens, and how far we have yet to go.

Rosemary's nephew, Anthony Shriver, credited her with the most significant life of all in a family of overachievers: "The interest [Rosemary] sparked in my family towards people with special needs will one day go down as the greatest accomplishment that any Kennedy has made."

ONE OFFSHOOT of the Education for All Handicapped Children Act was the creation of Rifton, the adaptive equipment company where I work as general manager. Rifton would not exist had it not been for those advocates, working often in isolation, sometimes in concert, to agitate for change. We

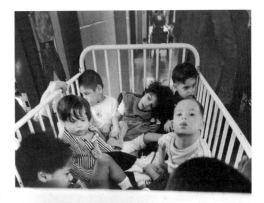
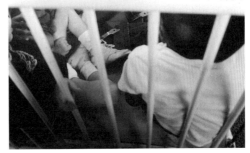

were fortunate to be well-situated to catch the wave of reform that demanded better treatment and dignity for persons with disabilities.

Since 1953 the Bruderhof communities had been operating a children's furniture and toy company called Community Playthings; by the 1970s there was a loyal customer base among public schools and nurseries. When Congress acted to have children moved out of institutions into the public school system, Community Playthings almost immediately started receiving urgent requests for adaptive chairs that might accommodate new students with special needs.

The Bruderhof's Deer Spring community was in rural Norfolk, Connecticut, home to several small institutions that provided residential care for children with disabilities. Ann Storck's Nursery, Ann's Nursery for Babies, and the Laurel School were visited regularly by the young people of Deer Spring, who came to sing, chaperone children on outings, or play with them on the premises.

Eight children at Willowbrook State School sit crammed into a single crib while waiting to receive physical therapy (1972).

Jerry Voll, who with his wife joined the Bruderhof in 1971, had studied to become a pastor but found himself working in the Community Playthings factory at Deer Spring, assembling wooden storage lockers, bookshelves, chairs, and similar school furnishings. He was just beginning to participate in discussions about diversifying the Bruderhof's business enterprises when he met Kevin Purcell, an employee of Connecticut's Department of Developmental Services who had come to Norfolk's school system to establish a program for newly mainstreamed children with disabilities. Purcell came knocking at the Deer Spring factory and teamed up with Voll to create better seating and positioning equipment: Their first collaborative creation was the "fully adjustable" Rifton E50 Chair. Remembering those early prototypes, Voll grins wryly at the ungainly combinations of slotted plywood and plastic knobs that characterized them. Then a youth group leader, he remembers that "the high schoolers at Deer Spring never tired of teasing me about those 'fully adjustable' chairs."

Jerry Voll

But they worked. Then therapy staff from Ann's Nursery helped develop a bath chair; standing frames followed. Voll started traveling further afield, harnessing the eagerness of therapists to contribute design input. He was joined in his efforts by others at Community Playthings, not only at the Deer Spring factory but at the Woodcrest community in Rifton, New York, which specialized in aluminum fabrication, and at New Meadow Run, in Farmington, Pennsylvania, which did commercial sewing. Wilmot Durgin and Van Geiger, two of the CPS volunteers who had raised the alarm in the 1940s, had by this point joined the Bruderhof and contributed their skills to the new endeavor. Durgin was one of the first to join Voll's efforts; his work

helped create Rifton's first prone stander prototype.

In 1977, the Community Playthings catalog included a four-page spread showcasing the new offerings. By 1980 the Rifton product line had expanded enough to justify its own catalog. Jerry Voll describes the moment when he helped the first user, a ten-year-old girl waiting with her parents in a school gym, into the newly designed Adjustable Walker. "We placed her in the walker, her first time upright and able to propel herself independently, and she took off across the gym floor. There was not a dry eye in the room."

SINCE THEN, Rifton's work has taken it into schools and hospitals and homes across the United States and to dozens of countries around the world. Rifton staff have had the privilege of working with people such as Linda Bidabe, who founded the MOVE Program and profoundly influenced Rifton's product designs, and Hiroyasu Itoh, the father of the disability rights movement in Japan. In my own time at Rifton I have met countless dedicated therapists, aides, teachers, parents, siblings, and others who understand that our society is richer to the degree that we care for our vulnerable members.

Indeed, this is perhaps the single most important lesson our country could acknowledge, that providing decent care for those in greatest need is not a sacrifice, something that slows our progress; it is a path to wholeness.

What does that look like?

Well, it looks like the Center for Disability Services (CFDS), a nonprofit agency in Albany, 160 miles up the Hudson from the now-shuttered Willowbrook. Compare the footage captured by Geraldo Rivera almost fifty years ago to the video of Octavius, a young boy whose life was saved by CFDS and who receives care and attention that would have been

unheard of even twenty-five years ago. That care includes world-class medical attention coupled with the strong sense, shared by the entire staff, that every child has the capacity for growth and development, in cognition and in independent movement. Everyone at the Center is involved, from the janitor to the senior therapist. They know that every moment of the day is an opportunity to learn.

The Center also designs its program to encourage active participation and respect the dignity of each child. Part of this design is using equipment that enables children to be upright and gives them agency to make their own choices and direct their own movements rather than be pushed in a wheelchair by an aide. Especially as children reach young adulthood, it also includes gear that can make it possible to use the toilet in private rather than face the indignity of being diapered in public or behind a curtain. These design choices protect individuals' autonomy and self-respect.

This approach has profound implications for the entire family of a person with special needs. Countless times I've heard heart-breaking stories of parents who day in and day out lift their child from a wheelchair into a car or onto a commode or into a tub,

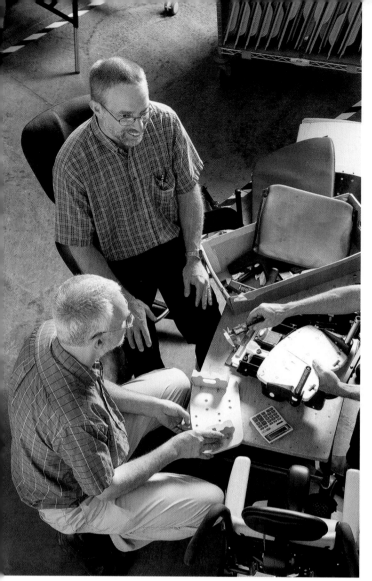

Sam Durgin, *top*, is the son of Wilmot Durgin and a designer at Rifton.

knowing that with each passing year their ability to perform these lifts is eroding. Their aging backs are no match for their children's growth, and they wonder, "Who will do this once we can no longer?" I have seen relief flood their faces when they see what the right equipment can do for their children, teaching them to bear weight, to stand upright, to pivot in place, and often – most powerfully – to walk independently.

But one major obstacle remains for far too many families. Because of America's patchwork healthcare and health insurance systems, getting coverage for needed medical care and equipment can be excruciatingly onerous. I

hear many desperate stories of months-long struggles to get insurance companies, private or public, to approve coverage for life-changing equipment. I hear stories of insurance denials that are mindless at best, heartless at worst. I also hear about the unique terror associated with the "disability cliff," that abrupt change in funding streams for all services that occurs, usually at age twenty-two, when a disabled adult is no longer eligible for special education under the public school system.

We drastically need a different national solution that will make services available for those without insurance coverage or sufficient private funds. So while we celebrate the progress we've made, we are constantly reminded there is still far to go. Closing institutional hellholes was one among many battles for the rights and dignity of the disabled. But we have hope; it comes from the small army of clinicians, technicians, and aides who work outside the public eye delivering care.

When we witness situations that offend our sensibilities we can choose to turn our heads or to speak out. My own small efforts at advocacy today draw their strength and purpose from those who went before us, people like Durgin or Geiger who acted in the shadows, or like Rivera and the Kennedys who reached a national audience. Neither Durgin nor Geiger, toiling in those remote human warehouses, could have known their solitary protests would have lasting effect. But surely both would have marveled at the thread running through decades, connecting their youthful outrage to the Bruderhof, which they both joined, and to Rifton, where they helped craft equipment to improve the lives of people with disabilities.

That thread extends to the present. In a happy coincidence, I find myself today working alongside Durgin's youngest son Sam, himself disabled from birth, who is a brilliant product designer. ➤

Spaces for Every Body

What would a world designed for humans with and without disabilities look like?

LEAH LIBRESCO SARGEANT

ADAPTIVE TECHNOLOGY and design make bridges. Ramps sloping gently down from a door, spaces set aside at the airport for nursing mothers, eye-tracking cameras that translate the smallest movements into computer-spoken words – these adjustments make the world more accessible to people who might otherwise be excluded.

Adaptive technology also creates a border. It indicates who is *not* expected to be a user of a tool, a space, a voice. Adaptive design is the complement to design for the *expected* person, the typical person, the person society readily recognizes as a full person. In two recent books, *What Can a Body Do: How We Meet the Built World* (Sara Hendren) and *Making Disability Modern: Design Histories* (essays edited by Bess Williamson and Elizabeth Guffey), the authors catalog the ways society is shaped to be exclusive, and how people who are initially excluded reclaim the space and dignity they are due.

An outdoor staircase in Robson Park, Vancouver, incorporates a ramp for wheelchairs and strollers.

Hendren, an artist who teaches design for disability at Olin College of Engineering, opens her book with a design challenge she posed to her students: Take Amanda, an art historian who is a Little Person, standing just over four feet tall. In her work as a curator, she travels and gives talks at museums, and she wants a customized lectern that suits her stature. She lays out a full set of design constraints: she wants to be able to carry and set it up by herself, it has to be strong enough to support a laptop, and it has to be robust enough for repeated use.

For a certain kind of designer, Amanda's request is superfluous. There is already a simpler solution – she can stand on a box. Indeed, many speaking venues keep a box on hand, not for Little People, but for women, as my parish did for women lectors who otherwise wouldn't quite reach a podium designed with the median man's height in mind. It was a solution Amanda had repeatedly relied on, and one she decided she was finished with. As Hendren explains, "She

The Swany bag acts as an unobtrusive mobility aid.

wanted to be able to do the speaking her job entailed without a device that required her to enact the repeated awkwardness of bringing her body to the dimensions of a room at odds with her physicality."

There is a profound gap between adaptive design that is intended to put an atypical or disabled user in the position of the typical user and one that treats her as a guest in her own right, anticipated and welcomed as she is.

One woman Hendren profiles, Cindy, is a quadruple amputee who has "some broad grasping function on one side, but no complete fingers at all." Like many people with disabilities, she has become a designer by necessity. She has the benefit of access to a state-of-the-art prosthetic, a black myoelectric hand with dozens of preprogrammed grip patterns for its delicately articulated fingers. But most of the time she leaves it in a drawer.

The drawer handle is adorned with one of the cable ties she has attached all over her house. While a conventional drawer pull anticipates a conventional hand, Cindy has added fixtures that are suited to what *her* hand can do. Most of her adaptations are cheap and "would never merit coverage in the shiny 'innovation' pages of the tech magazines." But each meets Cindy where she is *now* rather than being aimed at returning her to the same ways in which she moved through the world before her amputations.

ADAPTIVE TECHNOLOGY that aspires to fully restoring "typical" use can suit some disabled users. But, as Caroline Lieffers points out in "Artificial Limbs on the Panama Canal," in *Making Disability Modern*, it is also a way of deciding what ways of being

---

Leah Libresco Sargeant, a Plough *contributing editor, is the author of* Arriving at Amen *and* Building the Benedict Option. *Her writing has appeared in the* New York Times, First Things, *and* FiveThirtyEight.

society is willing to count as human, and what it counts as harm. In the first decade of the twentieth century, the Panama Canal project contracted with A. A. Marks, a manufacturer of prosthetics, to provide limbs for men injured at work there. The blithe advertisements juxtaposed the limbs and the canal as two forms of the triumph of human ingenuity over nature. What explosives and machinery destroyed, A. A. Marks prosthetics could replace.

Lieffers compares this response from canal administrators to "what scholar Jasbir Puar has, in a different context, labeled the imperialist's 'right to maim,'" which they complemented "with a medical-technological 'right to fix' on terms most favorable to their metropolitan interests." The limbs were (usually) sufficient to return men to work, and any other suffering was outside the scope of what the canal administrators thought of as their duty to redress.

The Department of Defense–sponsored Warrior Games live in a similarly uneasy space. The annual event "celebrates the resiliency and dedication of wounded, ill, and injured active duty and veteran US military service members," and the remarkable athletic performances are a testament to the determination of the participating soldiers. But the celebration also serves the story that injuries are fixable and transcendable. It deflects questions of whether these sacrifices were demanded in a just cause. When a sprinter runs on a carbon-fiber blade, the prosthetic is assisting a certain narrative, as well as a certain kind of excellence.

For some people with the need for assistance, telling the story of a return to normality is as essential as the physical support a device can provide. Cara Kiernan Fallon, in her essay "Walking Cane Style and Medicalized Mobility," explores how the common use of canes and walking sticks as fashion statements in the late nineteenth century created a blurry boundary between the able-bodied and the disabled. When everyone carried a walking stick, it was easier to age gracefully, gradually putting more weight on the stick for support. There was no harsh, visible transition to a walker or a medicalized cane – neither of which has the whimsy or personality of a walking stick.

In one of the final essays of *Making Disability Modern*, "Designing the Japanese Walking Bag," collection editor Elizabeth Guffey discusses her own experience with a kind of successor to the cane, similarly invisible in its ubiquity: the Swany bag. Businessman and polio survivor Etsuo Miyoshi noticed how much he felt steadied by a rolling suitcase, and designed the Swany bag as a mobility aid that appeared to be a similar bag. In order to launch the product in 1999, he was open about his own struggles, appearing in advertisements at a time when disability in Japan was often a private, shameful fact.

His openness helped the bag find its users, many of whom became amateur designers, speaking from their own need and prompting the company to add useful features like a wheel brake, a small fold-out seat, and a way to slim the profile of the bag for crowded interiors. But some of the feedback was less about users' struggles with the bag and more about their struggles with the society they moved through. "Swany's user feedback also alluded to perceptions of disability and fears of marginalization," Guffey writes. "Too often, customers

Books reviewed in this article

Sara Hendren, *What Can a Body Do?* (Riverhead Books, 2020) illustrated edition.

Bess Williamson and Elizabeth Guffey, eds., *Making Disability Modern* (Bloomsbury Visual Arts, 2020).

wrote, 'in a quiet residential area, the sound of the casters is loud.'" The already quiet wheels were dampened into near-silence. But, as Guffey points out, it was implausible that the low rattle of a wheel was truly disruptive: what users feared was that their presence was. They wanted a bag that would let them pass through, invisible and unremarked.

Assistive technology design can take into account these desires, but there is always something bitter about satisfying them. The pressure the visibly disabled face to "pass" as typical is real, but it is an unjust demand. It may relieve strain on an individual to help her hide, but the fear or disgust the able-bodied feel is poisonous to their own souls and requires purgation and healing, even if it is not outwardly expressed.

AND, OF COURSE, not everyone can succeed in passing as independent or able-bodied. In another essay, "The Ideology of Designing for Disability," Guffey follows the work of Selwyn Goldsmith, a research architect in Norwich, England, in the mid-twentieth century. He was familiar with the accepted best practices for design for the disabled, but, as he began interviewing the individual disabled people of his city, he found many of them were left out of the picture of the "typical atypical" person.

Guffey writes, "Of the almost three hundred people he initially interviewed, Goldsmith found that only six resembled [the] typical wheelchair user, that is, people who were 'able to go out and use public buildings independently.'" Instead, the wheelchair users he met often relied on caregivers for help. A ramp-accessible building and toilet – even one wide enough for a wheelchair – was still unusable for them if it didn't have space for two people to collaborate.

Goldsmith's interviews informed the substantial revisions he made to his second edition of *Designing for the Disabled* in 1967.

He rejected an American-popularized ideal of designing in order to allow the disabled to maneuver independently. Instead, he wanted to be able to anticipate disabled users as tightly enmeshed in a social fabric of support. Meeting their needs meant leaving room for the people they depended on. He no longer wanted to seamlessly integrate facilities for the disabled into typical facilities, but to be unafraid to label them visibly and call attention to their difference. He saw this not just as a design philosophy, but as a moral question on "evaluation of human worth."

Hendren finds similar themes underlying the stories and designs she profiles. Dependence "always implicates far more than one person," she writes. "Dependence creates relationships of necessary care – care that may be undertaken by individuals, families, local communities and municipal organizations, churches and mosques and temples, states or nations, or all of those in some mix." Being part of this tapestry of needs and care is not limited to the people regarded as disabled. As Hendren writes, "states of dimensional dependence from our infancy through the end of life might be the central fact of having a body, or rather *being* a body."

The experience of disability and dependence is not foreign to any of us, no matter how able-bodied or well-accommodated we are at present. Journalist Sara Luterman, who specializes in disability policy, politics, and culture, sees "independence as an illusion." I asked her how she helps her readers find points of connection to very different life experiences. Though we all fall somewhere on the spectrum of dependence, the temporary need of a pregnant mother may feel very different than the experience of growing up with a congenital limb difference, which is itself very different from finding one's way into Deafness late in life due to Ménière's disease.

Luterman starts with a simple proposition: "Everyone has the same fundamental needs, more or less. We all need food, we all need shelter, we all need social connection. We all need to feel like our lives are meaningful; we all need to feel pleasure sometimes."

Her goal isn't to ask the reader what it would be like to *be* the person at the heart of a reported story, but to imagine what it would be like to be denied what disabled people are denied. "It's not imagining what it would be like to be intellectually disabled," she tells me, "but what it would be like to be paid less than minimum wage."

T HELPS SIMPLY TO SEE the world built around us as not wholly given, but as the result of the choices made by specific, limited sets of people. As a parent, I return to the image of a set of enormous furniture constructed by artists Michael Seo, Cindy Jian, and Marie Applegate, which gave adults the perspective of children moving through a world not constructed to their scale. You might have the pleasure of walking under a table (and seeing an unexpected place for decoration) but you also suddenly find yourself unable to join others for a meal without a boost. Most of the built world excludes children's exploration and assumes they are being supervised and assisted by an adult.

In both *What Can a Body Do?* and *Making Disability Modern*, there are examples of other liminal spaces, where a "typical" person can enter an environment that is centered around the needs of a different experience. Near Gallaudet University, Hendren visits a "Signing Starbucks," which carries the principles of DeafSpace architecture over into the "regular" world. Everything is laid out to facilitate the lines of sight that signers depend on. The baristas are ready to accommodate Hendren and other non-signers, but it is still a place

Instructions are repeated in braille on a ticket-validating machine at a train station in Portland, Oregon.

where her defaults are foreign – an embassy from another world.

Two Dutch communities for the disabled operate spaces where their residents touch the outside world. De Hogeweyk is a village catering to patients with dementia, and Het Dorp is a town designed for the physically disabled. In a small business district in Het Dorp and in the restaurant of De Hogeweyk, people native to the "typical" world can enter, mingle, and step through a portal into an alternate world – a world that takes a different human experience as the pattern for "standard."

These spaces offer immersion; the two books are travelers' guides. Both help all of us, whatever our specific needs, to be more attentive to the work of translation and adaptation required to enter the allegedly public sphere. Each of us can look at the places where we are already well accommodated. We can ask where our community requires us to do the work to construct the comfort others enjoy effortlessly. We have the opportunity to smooth the way for the friends and neighbors we have, and to feel the absence of the potential friends or neighbors who are excluded by the communities we built. ➤

Mass shootings have
made violent death
seem normal. It's not.

The Lion's Mouth

EDWIDGE DANTICAT

A FEW YEARS AGO, on the eve of Christmas Eve, I headed to the nearby Aventura Mall to get my daughter Mira her first cellphone. The line to drive into the mall was endless. It was, I suspected, filled with people like me, who could no longer get anything on the internet that would be delivered before Christmas. The line at the store was also long, but not as long as the winding line of cars heading for the exit of the five-story parking structure after I had purchased the phone. I had felt lucky to have found a parking spot on the top floor when I arrived, but now I felt cursed. At the pace the cars were moving, I worried that I might still be sitting in my car on Christmas morning.

Just as I neared the second floor, I saw dozens of people racing into the parking structure. Among the many screams and voices was one of a woman calling for someone named Jackson. In the surreal way that one's mind works at a time like this, I remember thinking, for a second, that she was calling the deceased singer Michael Jackson. Later I realized that had I been shot right then and there, my final thought on this earth would have been of Michael Jackson.

The crowd rushing past my car and the other cars stuck in the parking lot made driving out impossible.

"What's going on?" I shouted at the people sprinting past.

The same question echoed from the mouths of other drivers both in front and behind me.

"There's a shooter in the mall!" many of the fleeing said.

The pace of events quickened as people began to shout "Run! Run!" even as they were already running. It was obvious then that I too

Carlos Antonio Rancaño, *The Delicate Fight*, oil on canvas, 2020

Edwidge Danticat is the author of many books, including, most recently, Everything Inside: Stories (Knopf, 2019).

would have to run. The cars were at a standstill. Many of the drivers ahead of me had already abandoned their vehicles. I quickly turned off my car then put the keys – and that darn phone – in my purse. Then I heard a series of loud explosions echo through the parking lot. To my panicked ears, it sounded like bombs were going off nearby. Suddenly there were many more of

---

These days, our children not only read about dying violently, or see it on the internet, but they are also being trained to expect it, anticipate it, and even plan for it.

us sprinting, running, dashing, more abandoned cars, and more parents screaming their children's names. It was hard to tell as I weaved my way through a crowd of fleeing people, and unmoving cars, whether I was escaping or heading toward these explosions.

My adrenaline took over and I ran down the parking lot ramp until I was on the ground floor and outside. At the parking lot exit were several heavily armed police officers headed in the direction I'd just come from. This reminded me of the stories I'd heard after September 11, 2001, of first responders going into the World Trade Center as others ran out.

I was still hearing the explosions, which made me wonder whether the active shooter, or shooters, might not also be snipers who could be waiting to pick off the fleeing from the roofs of the many stores surrounding us. So I found a bush on the side of the parking structure and took cover there. The bush was part of a low hedge that was meant to soften the look of the

parking structure concrete. I squeezed myself in between that hedge and the wall to catch my breath.

People were still running, still fleeing the mall. More police and emergency vehicles were coming in too. After a few minutes behind the hedge, I joined a group of shoppers heading toward a footbridge that led to the main road outside. Everyone was out of breath, all of us, walking again – and not running – for the first time since fleeing the mall. Then the flood of cell phone calls began. Many were still frantic. Some had left behind loved ones, who as far as they knew were caught up in a massacre.

My husband was with our two daughters at a holiday theme park called Santa's Enchanted Forest. I texted him to let him know I was safe. I then went on Twitter and entered the words "Aventura Mall" in the search box. The first tweet I saw was written by Jacqueline Charles, a *Miami Herald* reporter, who happened to be in the mall hiding inside a storeroom closet with dozens of other people. I then called my niece who lived nearby. When she and her husband arrived, I got in their car, collapsed in the back seat, and burst into tears.

I was already counting the numbers in my head. Judging from the size of the mall and the booming explosions I'd heard, I believed that dozens of people had already died. I imagined the headlines and the breaking news banners. This one, I thought, would probably be called "The Christmas Massacre."

IT TURNED OUT TO BE a hoax, the most recent in a series at Florida malls. Jacqueline Charles learned that some young people had perpetrated it with an app that made the sounds of gunshots and bomb detonations, which were then amplified by speakers. In a few of the similar hoaxes, firecrackers were used to cause panic so that criminals could rob the stores.

When I first learned there hadn't really been a massacre, I felt lucky, but also angry. Then I began making jokes. My greatest shame, I told my niece, would have been dying clutching that damned phone. As soon as I was reunited with my family, my mother-in-law reminded me how I had worried that Santa's Enchanted Forest, a place filled with hundreds of distracted children and adults, much like the mall, might be a "soft target," in modern terrorism or school-shooter speak. Still both my husband and I had kept to our plans. After all, these things always seemed to happen in other places, and to other people.

With every passing year, we accrue more formidable accounts of what it's like to actually survive one of those massacres. The harrowing testimonies of the survivors of the shooting at Parkland, Florida's Marjory Stoneman Douglas High School, where seventeen people died and seventeen others were wounded, the grace and eloquence of these young advocates, their efforts to include less privileged young people – including some young people of color, whose communities are chronically and disproportionately affected by gun violence – has been incredibly moving for me, especially as my daughters are approaching their age. As one of my daughter's middle school teachers said when we went to our local March for Our Lives rally the day before her thirteenth birthday, this generation lives in great proximity to graphic, vivid trauma and pain. Yet they are also gifted and motivated enough and have enough tools and platforms to share that pain with the rest of us. These days, our children not only read about dying violently, or see it on the internet, or act it out, as some do, in video games, but they are also being trained to expect it, anticipate it, and even plan for it. One of the signs I found most striking at the rally was carried by an African American girl who reminded me of my

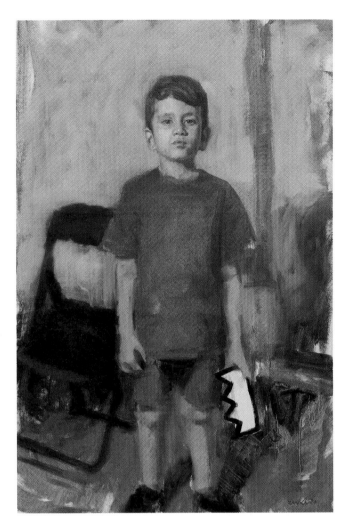

younger daughter. Her sign simply read, "LET US GROW UP!"

Over time, I have come to think of my experience at Aventura Mall as a kind of drill, one not unlike the ones carried out at my daughters' school and at many other schools around the United States. Soon after the Marjory Stoneman Douglas High School shooting, my daughters came home, each describing her own experience of the active shooter drill at their school. My younger daughter, Leila, was told to hide under her desk, which is wooden and small and even she realized would not protect her from an assault rifle. My older daughter, Mira, was told that if she happened to find herself in the hallway with the shooter nearby, she should find an unlocked classroom and run

Carlos Antonio Rancaño, *King In I*, oil on canvas, 2021

Carlos Antonio Rancaño, *Princess*, oil on canvas, 2019

how to keep my daughters alive in a way I might still be able to control. I also hoped that it would offer some guidance about mental and psychological survival, how not to let your soul die either. Though the lettuce-shaped letters on the book cover signaled its true content, I also wanted it around to remind me that death is something one can willingly put off for a little while.

I have spent a lot of time thinking about death and dying since that day, but even before that, since my mother died of ovarian cancer in 2014. As a writer, part of my job is to wrestle with mortality, both my own and that of others. I do this by writing about fictional people I give life to, throw untold atrocities at, then either redeem or destroy. In my own life, one way I wrestle with mortality is by keeping a pocket-size notebook with a list of instructions and counsel for my daughters, ranging from what they might call cringey ("Do not ever underestimate how awesome you are") to the spiritual ("Keep some element of faith in your life – you saw how your grandmother's faith brought her such solace and comfort as she was dying"). This, too, I took from my mother. The day she died, on the nightstand by her bed, I found an advice-filled cassette created for my three brothers and me. On the tape, she told us not to be too sad, since she'd lived a long and fulfilling life, as well as what I should wear to her funeral: a long-sleeved black dress, a hat, no open-toe shoes. That cassette, I now realize, is one of the ways she resisted dying.

As a terminal cancer patient, my mother understood quite well how not to die, even when you *must* die. Her tranquil yet firm voice on that cassette proves it. She knew we would be listening to her advice about the kind of clothes we should wear to her funeral and the way we should discipline our children long after she was gone. She still wanted to parent us from the grave.

inside. Since her class had been advised to lock the door, I told her to run instead to the nearest bathroom or supply closet and take cover there instead. I hoped that wasn't stupid, potentially deadly advice.

I HAVE A VERY FAT BOOK on my bedside table called *How Not to Die* by Michael Greger, a physician and nutritionist, and Gene Stone. It explains in great detail how not to die from different ailments, ranging from heart disease to cancer, mainly by eating a plant-based diet and by exercising. It does not tell you, however, how not to die from school or mall shootings, or police brutality, or racialized vigilante violence.

I picked up the book from the front table of my local independent bookstore soon after my experience at Aventura Mall. I was hoping it could counsel me on how to stay alive and

At the end of my mother's life, when we were constantly telling each other stories, I told her how I'd once read that rice came to our part of the world – the Caribbean – from the African continent, because an enslaved woman had hidden some grains in her hair. I'm not sure whether this story is true or not, but it is one of many stories about both food and our communal past that I love.

"You mean her scalp was a garden?" my mother asked incredulously, even as her own scalp became more exposed as a side effect of chemotherapy.

The woman with the rice in her hair, I realize, was imagining a future in which she would exist in some other way than in her own flesh. She was trying to figure out not only how not to die, but how the people who would come after her would survive.

I AM ON THE ADVISORY BOARD of an organization called Exchange for Change, which offers writing workshops at several Florida prisons. Twice a year, Exchange for Change holds a ceremony for the incarcerated students who have participated in the program. The last one I attended, before the onset of Covid-19, was at Dade Correctional Institution, a men's facility.

Florida has one of the United States' largest prison populations, which is primarily made up of people of color. The mural-covered cinder-block visitation room where the graduation took place reflects this too, though all the men were wearing the same color: blue. Exchange for Change offers classes ranging from memoir, essay, poetry, and graphic-novel writing to a Shakespeare performance class. The work of the incarcerated writers is always deeply felt, raw, and heart-wrenching. Their writing is filled with references to freedom, redemption, injustice, restitution, regrets,

mistakes, and second chances, even as the readings and performances are interrupted by head counts and the buzz of the correctional staff's two-way radios. Theirs is the urgent kind of writing one comes up with while trying to keep a body and soul alive. Some of the incarcerated writers have little hope of ever living

---

As a writer, part of my job is to wrestle with mortality, both my own and that of others.

outside prison walls, yet they want their words to journey beyond the layers of barbed wire around them, beyond even themselves.

"Our pen is our penicillin," the emcee, poet Eduardo "Echo" Martinez, said. "We are always trying to find the balance between becoming a man and an animal – a manimal."

The Shakespeare class wrestled with questions of legacy and humanity, life and death. Some through Hamlet's famous soliloquy:

> To be, or not to be, that is the question:
> Whether 'tis nobler in the mind to suffer
> The slings and arrows of outrageous
>   fortune,
> Or to take arms against a sea of troubles,
> And by opposing end them.
> To die – to sleep . . .

Or Mark Antony's in *Julius Caesar*:

> Friends, Romans, countrymen, lend me
>   your ears . . .
> The evil that men do lives after them;
> The good is oft interred with their bones . . .

This, I realized, is how these incarcerated writers were trying desperately not only to keep their bodies and souls alive, but to expand beyond themselves, to grow.

Carlos Antonio Rancaño, *Beyond the Horizon*, oil on canvas, 2019

raise one's children, and pay the rent, and wrestle with one's mortality.

While sitting between that hedge and the wall at Aventura Mall that Christmas Eve's eve, I thought I felt the fetid jaws of the lion's mouth around my neck, and I momentarily surrendered. With the possibility of dying feeling so actual, and so real, I was reminded yet once again that in the midst of life, we are in death, especially when death becomes so commonplace that even the youngest among us are watching their peers die, or are hearing about others dying, or are rehearsing not to die, as though they were warriors, fighters in battles and wars.

I keep thinking back to the young African American girl at the March for Our Lives rally, the one, among many, who was carrying a sign that read, "LET US GROW UP!" I want to make that plea for her and for my daughters too, whether it be from school or mall shootings, or police brutality, or racialized vigilante violence: Please, let them grow up. And for the adults among us, let's keep growing. ⤳

"The Lion's Mouth" is adapted from the Brooklyn Public Library "Message from the Library" lecture presented on June 17, 2018.

I N *THE DEVIL FINDS WORK,* James Baldwin's 1976 book-length essay examining life via films, he wrote:

It is a terrible thing, simply, to be trapped in one's history, and attempt, in the same motion (and in this, our life!) to accept, deny, reject, and redeem it – and, also, on whatever level, to profit from it. And: with one's head in the fetid jaws of this lion's mouth, attempt to love and be loved, and

Editors' Picks

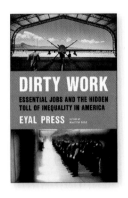

Dirty Work
Essential Jobs and
the Hidden Toll
of Inequality in
America

Eyal Press
(Farrar, Straus & Giroux)

Prisoners abound in this tour de force, but few are criminals. They are simply hapless men and women trapped in a system that counts on them to carry out tasks most of us cannot imagine doing ourselves, in places as varied as slaughterhouses, military drone-operating offices, and the control units of America's grimmest prisons.

Eyal Press, a reporter who combines hard data and analysis with unsettling anecdotes, is a storyteller in the tradition of the best muckrakers. What makes his book especially urgent is the fact that the beleaguered people he profiles belong to a largely invisible and therefore forgotten workforce.

While an ongoing pandemic has highlighted the contributions of "essential" workers and given them a brief (and bittersweet) taste of fame, no one will ever celebrate the people in *Dirty Work*. There are no unsung heroes here – no teachers, nurses, or first responders. What little we know of their work makes us look at them askance, if not treat them with opprobrium. And yet, as Press shows, their jobs are vital to the running of our economy.

Press's subjects are not self-pitying victims, but they do find their jobs demeaning and even morally compromising. Guilt often haunts them. One, a prison psychologist named Harriet, personally witnesses the degradation of inmates – and spends sleepless nights wondering whether she is another casualty of the system or its enabler. Why doesn't she blow the whistle on what's happening? Like many who subsist on lower rungs of the socioeconomic ladder, she lives in fear of being fired, and so does her best to suppress her conflicted emotions. Given the financial insecurity that forced her into accepting her position in the first place, she sees few other options for employment.

So, are people like Harriet guilty or not? It's a question most of us never have to ask, relying as we do on the sacrifices others make so that we can breathe easy at night: violent criminals safely locked away, steaks at the ready in every supermarket, terrorists taken down in some high-stakes intelligence operation overseas.

For most of us, the dirty work others do is a necessary evil, apt to elicit little more than a passing thought. After all, when it is hidden behind institutional walls, it's easier to rationalize or ignore. We *expect* prisons and sweatshops to be places of despair. And if the people who work there weren't willing to carry out their tasks, wouldn't others have to?

In a 1927 essay titled "The Individual and World Need," Eberhard Arnold argues that collective guilt is an "inevitability" and proposes that "confessing" our personal co-responsibility for what is wrong in the world is a crucial step to becoming fully human. Eyal Press invites us to do precisely that: not just to educate ourselves, but to move from apathy toward compassion – the word means "to suffer with." *Dirty Work* shows how our fortunes are inextricably linked with others' fates. As long as we continue to turn a blind eye to their lot, we do so at their expense and our own.

—*Chris Zimmerman*

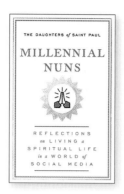

Millennial Nuns
Reflections on Living a Spiritual Life in a World of Social Media

The Daughters of Saint Paul
(Tiller Press)

There is a received wisdom in the consecrated religious life that a community is flourishing and healthy if each of its members is clearly and unapologetically an individual – and, moreover, encouraged to be so. *Millennial Nuns*, the reflections of eight young professed sisters of the Daughters of Saint Paul, bears clear testament to this wisdom. An engaging collection of personal essays exploring what it means to be a religious sister in the twenty-first century, this book has something to offer both to those discerning

Eight millennial women tell why they ended up in a convent.

the religious life and those merely curious about it – even if it sidesteps some deeper and more thorny questions about how to pursue a contemplative life in a frantically online world.

The Daughters of Saint Paul are a Roman Catholic order founded in 1915 by James Alberione. Their apostolate, or mission, is focused on the preaching of the gospel through modern media. At the time of their founding this meant newspapers and the radio, but now encompasses YouTube, Instagram, and podcasting, to name but a few of the media platforms on which the sisters are active.

The eight sisters who contributed to the book all evidently belong to a community with a charism of preaching: each is an appealing writer with a strong and distinctive style. There is a broad – presumably deliberately so – mix of ethnic, social, and professional backgrounds represented, and a no-nonsense honesty about the difficulties both of discerning a vocation to the religious life and of living it out. Their stories will satisfy the curiosity of those who want to know how millennial women end up in convents and of those who want to know what it is they do once they're in there. It also has something to offer to those who know little about Catholicism more generally: at several points the sisters take time to explain points of doctrine or devotional practices.

The book promises to "appeal to any reader looking to discover more about balancing faith with the modern age," but readers looking for deeper insight on this topic will probably finish the book unsatisfied. I found that many of my own questions about how the Daughters of Saint Paul live out their preaching charism went unanswered. For instance: How does extensive use of social media impact the development of spiritual disciplines such as detachment and recollection? How does the community discern how much of their communal life to share online? Ultimately, for all its merits, *Millennial Nuns* only scratches the surface of what it means to commit oneself to Christ in a digital age; any reader wanting to find out more will need to do a little further reading, or maybe even meet some sisters and speak to them directly. Perhaps that isn't such a bad thing.

—*Sr. Carino Hodder, OP*

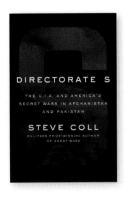

Directorate S
The C.I.A. and America's Secret Wars in Afghanistan and Pakistan

Steve Coll
(Penguin Press)

The historian Herodotus gave us the saying "circumstances rule men; men do not rule circumstances" to warn us away from the illusion that we are wise and powerful enough to make the world bend completely to our expectations.

The generals and CIA operatives who populate journalist Steve Coll's *Directorate S* would have done well to heed Herodotus' advice. Coll's hefty book picks up where his Pulitzer Prize–winning *Ghost Wars* left off, giving us the twisting story of top-secret operatives, both American and Pakistani, and the cat and mouse game (an obligatory phrase when writing about spies) played in reaction to the 9/11 attacks and the subsequent bid to control the Taliban and reshape Afghanistan. Afghanistan suffered through change, surely, but not in the way that American forces intended. After nearly two decades of violence and squandered resources, Coll attempts to give an at least provisional theory of why the cause was lost.

That means countless hours of interviews with people on the ground and massive document dumps alongside masterful control of a complex, sweeping narrative. Wars are such complicated endeavors that there's always something more to learn, always another fact to be recovered from the miasma of violence and degradation. One of the most shocking takeaways was how the Pakistani intelligence service, ISI, used its titular Directorate S to manipulate the Taliban by keeping them agitated enough to lure American forces into expanding a war which was, by 2004 at least, almost an afterthought to the action in Iraq.

As elucidating as *Directorate S* is, its real strength is the complexity of the human drama itself. Coll gives us portraits of the actual people wrapped up in this insane drama, from eccentric but skillful American operatives such as Rich Blee, the second-generation intelligence officer who had been warning higher-ups about an impending attack from Bin Laden, to Amrullah Selah, the boy-wonder intelligence chief of a northern tribe stuck in a vice grip

Why did the United States lose in Afghanistan?

between the Taliban, al-Qaeda, and the Americans. There's a literary majesty to the way Coll portrays this sad parade of tragic figures in tight spots, the rag dolls of fate.

And yet despite the ambitious scope of the book, there's something fundamental missing. Just as the Diagnostic and Statistical Manual of Mental Disorders doesn't contain a definition of sanity, *Directorate S* doesn't clearly articulate what our nation *should* have done. This isn't necessarily Coll's fault; he conveys by insinuation that hubris and overreach were baked into the project from its very beginnings, and that eventual failure is an unavoidable reality for every imperial project. Herodotus might have warned us of the outcome, but only a staggering and dramatic shift in how we conceive of nationality, power, and foreign affairs might have prevented it – or prevent it happening again.

—*Scott Beauchamp* ⤳

KELSEY OSGOOD

Stranger in a Strange Land

Even in Brooklyn, our Orthodox Jewish family feels alien.
That's not all bad.

ON OCTOBER 27, 2018, I was sitting at our synagogue's children's service on Shabbat morning, watching my toddler hug a miniature stuffed Torah, when my husband came into the room and whispered into my ear.

"There's been a shooting at a shul," he said. "The security guard is reading the news on his phone downstairs." This was the massacre at the Tree of Life Synagogue in Pittsburgh.

Our young family had recently relocated back to New York City from London. We'd signed a lease, sight unseen, on a duplex apartment in Brooklyn, only a five-minute walk to the closest Orthodox synagogue. Before we'd lived in London, my husband and I hadn't had much personal experience with feeling singled out as a result of our faith: we'd become gradually more religious as adults in New York, where it had been easy to forget how much of a minority we were, given the outsized impact on the culture of the city Judaism has had. Our social circle had reacted to our growing religiosity with a sort of benign confusion or indifference, which was usually fine, as we could count on those in our orbit to have at least a passing familiarity with Jewish practice.

But in London, where we'd amped up our ritual observance and where there are far fewer observant Jews, we'd fielded snide remarks from coworkers, found a lack of kosher restaurants, hiked twenty-five minutes to attend synagogue, which had a constant security presence, and noted passersby on the street staring at my husband's kippah. We were tired of feeling so isolated, and were anxious to take advantage of the Jewish offerings in Brooklyn, a borough where nearly a quarter of the residents are Jewish. Our new neighborhood was not overwhelmingly Jewish, like the tight-knit Hasidic enclaves nearby, but even still, we figured we were bound to feel far less alone. The day we officially moved in, I climbed up the little ladder onto the tiny roof deck and stood in the frigid night to gaze across at the Statue of Liberty – Emma Lazarus's "Mother of Exiles"– and listen to the boat horns bellow in the fog, a corny affection for my hometown, whose embrace was wide enough for everyone, swelling in my heart.

The idyll turned out to be mostly mirage. True, it was less of a schlep to get a kosher chicken in Brooklyn Heights than it had been in London's West End, but we still felt alone. Most of our Jewish neighbors were the type who measured Jewish authenticity by sense of humor and bagel order, rather than by commitment to Torah study or delight in the Sabbath (indeed, for this group, mild disdain for Jewish practice can be taken as a positive sign of Jewishness). Our synagogue was tiny, frequented by a largely older demographic, and not quite aligned with our beliefs as a family; the second closest Orthodox shul

Brooklyn's Williamsburg neighborhood. All photography by Paul McGeiver.

Kelsey Osgood is the author of How to Disappear Completely: On Modern Anorexia *and has written for the* New York Times, *the* New Yorker, Longreads, *and the* Washington Post. *She is currently working on a book about religious conversion among Millennial and Gen-Z women.*

was a forty-five-minute trek away. There were moments where I felt like our family was an oddity to be gawked at, such as when local college students would show up at our synagogue hoping to snap photos of our congregation worshiping in order to fulfill a class assignment, or when other parents on the playground would see my son's kippah (he started wearing one at a younger age than most boys) and make a point of telling me how their little Stephen also did Shabbat at his nursery school. "I'm listening to a podcast on the *parsha*" (weekly Torah portion), I once heard a mom stage-whisper to her child's babysitter (on Shabbat, for that matter, when use of electronics is prohibited), clearly for my benefit.

> **There are ways of convincing yourself you are at home, until the knowledge that you aren't becomes unavoidable.**

Yet these were harmless reminders of our fundamental outsiderness, I figured. Some were even endearing, and they were certainly preferable to apathy or disdain. When the Tree of Life shooting happened, I told myself that it was the work of a madman, no more an indication of the mainstream's attitude towards me than the Columbine shooters' actions reflected America's feelings about teenagers. But there are ways, it turns out, of convincing yourself you are at home, until the knowledge that you aren't becomes unavoidable.

On the Monday following the shooting, walking with my husband, I saw a swastika, crudely scrawled in yellow chalk on a house on our block.

"Look."

We stood there in shock, until we noticed a group of our neighbors gathered around a police officer. We learned that a few houses had been vandalized, but no one had seen anything.

A detective was on her way. Our neighbors didn't seem terribly worried: probably pranks in the name of Halloween, they shrugged. One by one, they drifted back indoors. I had to go relieve our babysitter, but my husband stayed behind. He was the only resident there when the detective arrived.

"Well, you're not a homeowner," she said, "so why are you so worked up about this?"

My son's first semi-cognizant Halloween was forty-eight hours away, but that was hardly cheering. Even without the swastika incident, I'd been dreading it. Some decades earlier, a family on our block had given out homemade doughnuts, drawing crowds of people from across Brooklyn. Though the family had long since left, the celebrants still came, forcing the police to shut down the street to traffic. This shouldn't have incited such handwringing: an all-American hullabaloo bound to entertain my rambunctious child for hours, dropped straight onto my doorstep! And yet the event brought up all sorts of anxiety for me about the life I was preparing my son for. In the religious Jewish world, Halloween is mostly just not done, but both my husband and I had grown up with it and emerged unscathed. Could I just view it as harmless fun? Or did everything in my life have to be *about* my Judaism? I felt like I was constantly singling out myself and my family as different – no, we can't eat that meat you just cooked in your non-kosher oven; no, we can't meet you for Saturday brunch; no, we can't join your Christmas celebrations – and it was awkward and tiring. I worried constantly that people felt like I was insulting them, or indeed, that I might actually *be* insulting them. I also worried about what I was teaching my child about the non-Jewish world. Was there ever a case where outlawing things might make them seem more alluring?

I hadn't yet then heard of the concept I was unwittingly grappling with, that of the *ger*

v'toshav, a person who is both a resident and an alien, or stranger. It's a phrase Avraham uses to describe himself in the portion of Genesis in which he's searching for a burial plot for Sarah. "I am (both) an alien and a citizen among you," he says to the Hittites who surrounded him in Hebron. (In the Torah, "ger" is one of three words that denotes foreigner, and of the three, connotes the most fondness and tolerance. Over the years, it etymologically developed to mean "convert.")

At first glance, it appears that the two are at odds with one another: how can one be both a citizen and an alien? But while the term eventually evolved to refer to righteous foreigners living within the Israelite nation, it also perfectly encapsulates the precarious position of the Jews, who for centuries have had to engage in a delicate dance of civic participation and cultural rejection in order to be good citizens while also maintaining their identity. It is a dance I engage in every day of my life, on behalf of my children, my family, and myself, one for which I often feel I don't know the steps at all, but dance it – haltingly, awkwardly, rapidly – I must. Ask me on any given day, and I'll tell you it is more rewarding than painful, more an act of agency than passivity, more assertive than defensive, more a net good than a loss. On others, I'll say the opposite.

FROM SOME OF THEIR earliest moments as a nation following the exodus from Egypt, the Jews were marked by G-d to remain separate: "For you are a people consecrated to the LORD your G-d," Moshe tells them, using the Hebrew *kadosh,* which implies both "holy" and "set apart." At times, this separation is framed as a blessing, bestowed upon the Jews by G-d because of his love for them; elsewhere, it's suggested that G-d separates the Jews so he can more readily discipline and punish them, the way a father might make an example of his eldest child. Throughout Deuteronomy and Leviticus, the major texts in which Moshe reveals G-d's laws to the Jews, some precepts are listed that explicitly decry intermingling – "You shall not intermarry with [the other nations]; do not give your daughters to their sons or take their daughters for your sons" – while other laws seem to produce Jewish isolation as a byproduct of adherence, such as those relating to dietary restrictions.

A parallel polis existed alongside the dominant cultures everywhere from Poland to Italy to Yemen, one with its own calendar, legal code, and rituals.

Over the centuries, some thinkers have claimed that separatism protects what is an intrinsic and heritable holiness, which any sustained contact with the non-Jewish world would desecrate or derail. ("The soul of the Gentiles comes from the three *klipot*: wind, cloud, and fire, all of them evil," wrote sixteenth-century mystic rabbi Isaac Luria. "So is the case with impure animals, beasts, and birds.") Others, like the contemporary Orthodox rabbi Nathan Lopes Cardozo, have argued that Biblical separatism was purely instrumental, designed to keep Jews from participating in the barbaric rituals associated with Biblical-era idolatry, such as human sacrifice and orgies. Now that this kind of paganism is virtually nonexistent, Rabbi Cardozo says, laws including the prohibition against drinking wine handled by a Gentile (lest it be used in such rituals) should be modified. This viewpoint is compelling, but viewed by Orthodoxy

as a whole as perilous: if we do away with *some* laws ensuring our survival as a group, then what's to stop us from discarding them all, thus all but guaranteeing complete assimilation and, ergo, dissolution?

The predominant middle-road view, espoused by thinkers from the Talmudic sage Rabbi Yehoshua to Maimonides to Chief Rabbi Lord Jonathan Sacks, is the spiritual equivalent of separate-but-equal: yes, Jews are different, and yes, their beliefs require some degree of segregation, but it doesn't mean they are better than others, or that non-Jews are unworthy of G-d's care and salvation. Indeed, many of this school say, there is ample evidence that Judaism believes all people can live dignified lives and have a place in eternity without sacrificing their own creeds. And yet knowing how separate-but-equal has been applied in other contexts, it's not hard to see how this rationale might seem unsettling, no matter how beautifully and gently framed.

After the destruction of the Second Temple and the exile from Israel, pilgrimages and burnt offerings were no longer possible; communal prayer and religious study had to suffice. Jewish enclaves in the diaspora formed geographically around synagogues and yeshivas; other institutions vital to Jewish life, like ritual baths and kosher butchers, naturally sprouted up alongside them. A parallel polis, as Czech dissident Vaclav Benda called it, existed alongside the dominant cultures everywhere from Poland to Italy to Yemen, one with its own calendar, legal code, and rituals. To this day, Jews have continued building "a fence around the Torah," to borrow a popular phrase and concept from the Rabbinic ethics text *Pirkei Avot*, both to more obviously signal the depth of their piety and as a means of protecting themselves against a hostile world. Jewish law, in the words of twentieth-century rabbi Eliezer Berkovits, became increasingly

"defensive": the prohibition against "round[ing] off the side-growth of your beard" led to the long sidelocks worn by Hasidic men, the seemingly simple instruction to not cook a kid in its mother's milk became *don't eat at your Gentile neighbor's house in case she once made chicken parmesan in her oven*, and the idea that a non-Jew shouldn't handle an open bottle of kosher wine lest she secretly sneak some for idolatrous purposes led to a thoroughly embarrassing moment for a friend in the middle of her conversion process: the host of a Shabbat meal tossed a bottle of Cabernet simply because she had glanced at it, despite no law that states a Gentile can contaminate a bottle of wine with a mere look.

Today, if you want to live an Orthodox life, you'll have to move to a parallel polis, as Orthodox communities remain concentrated because of the prohibition against driving on Shabbat. (The dramatic and ongoing decline of the Conservative movement in America can largely be traced back to its ill-fated decision to rule otherwise, thus inadvertently de-centralizing their communities and undermining their self-proclaimed identity as a law-based denomination.) You'll secure for your child a religious education, reside within walking distance of a synagogue, shop at kosher stores, fill your shelves with books from Jewish publishers, and so on and so forth. When it comes to exactly how separate one's polis is, though, there is a pretty wide spectrum. On the liberal end are the Modern Orthodox, like me. We often wear some distinctive garb, keep kosher, and generally reside in clusters, but give our children a secular education and partake of some mainstream culture. On the conservative end, there are the Haredim, who dress far more conspicuously, avoid secular media, and, in the case of Hasidim, speak Yiddish and eschew higher education. They are the stuff separatist dreams are made of. And yet, as ever, the reality is more complex.

WHEN I WAS IN my early twenties, and beginning the slow process of falling in love with Judaism, it was the Haredim I first became enamored with. If I found myself near a visibly Jewish man on the subway, I'd sidle up to peek at the religious text he was poring over on his commute. If I had to meet a friend in the hipster stronghold of Williamsburg, I'd forgo the subway ride

43

in favor of a walk through Hasidic South Williamsburg – anything to feel, for a precious twenty minutes or so, the sensation of being in a space purer than my own, even if it was still just a grimy stretch of city streets. There was a 1988 documentary I watched about a dozen times called *A World Apart* (an altogether too glowing and simplistic representation of Hasidic life, I later learned) that informed me that all Hasidim were in constant pursuit of *dveykus*, defined by the narrators as a "mystical state of cleaving to G-d," a state that could be reached not only by praying but by engaging in nearly any quotidian activity with the right amount of joy and concentration. By that point, I had lived most of my life without any connection to a divine source, following an abrupt rejection of religion at age eight. Walking through the neighborhood, I felt

like a starved person watching others feast at a banquet.

Having spent many hours in insular religious environments, both Jewish and not, in the course of writing about religion, I have discovered that I'm far from the only one guilty of romanticizing them. From the Amish to cloistered Catholics, the image of the devoted, isolated religious group often evokes dreamy ideas about authenticity, quality of attention, and wholesomeness, even from some hardened secularists. After all, such things are in short supply in mainstream American culture. And yet the reverie is usually simplistic to the point of delusion. When I tell people, for example, that even in conservative Amish communities, there exists a bordering ecosystem of non-Amish who interact with and in some ways prop up the community – "English" drivers who ferry the Amish around in vans, or visitor guides, or the hordes of tourists who pump money into the local economy – they wonder aloud if allowing another person to drive renders the Amish not "real." Once, when visiting Sabbathday Lake Shaker Village in Maine, I overheard a guide explain that the Shakers shop at Walmart to a group of visibly disappointed visitors. In that moment, I was instantly reminded of a hypothetical in Walker Percy's essay "The Loss of the Creature," part of his 1975 collection, *The Message in the Bottle*, in which Percy wonders what would happen when an American couple vacationing in Mexico, ecstatic at having discovered the perfect quaint Indigenous village, was confronted with a tribal chief brandishing a Sears catalog.

Nearly a decade ago, a friend and I traveled to New Square, a tiny Hasidic enclave north of New York City, to stay at the home of a local woman over Shabbat. We ate all our meals at the apartment of the fishmonger and watched the *tish* – a ritual meal in which the *rebbe* leads the men below in spirited song, sometimes until the wee hours of the morning – through the wooden slats of the women's balcony above, accompanied by three local teenagers who had taken us under their wings. While I felt rather constrained in my conversation with the local women, who seemed to only be able to discuss household cleaning and food preparation, I could still glimpse the charm of living in a contemporary *shtetl*, where everyone knew each other, and where the quieter rhythms of life were valued. I could, that is, until our companions smiled wryly and began talking about their clandestine Facebook accounts – something *I* didn't even have – and my vision of a standalone world was punctured yet again.

Once I realized that every faith community – from the Satmar Hasidim to the Swartzentruber Amish to the mainline Protestants to the Modern Orthodox – were negotiating the boundaries between tradition and modernity, that no fences constructed of the past were high enough to completely keep out our present, I ceased glorifying these places. I stopped believing that any individual or group could so fully purify their environments that they would not have to grapple with the questions people everywhere are asking of themselves: how much should the wider world intrude into my physical space, and into my soul? True, the more conservative communities might be able to hold off on some fronts for longer, but the world *will* come for them, too. *"Azoy vi es goyisht zich, azoy yiddisht zich,"* a friend who grew up in a Hasidic enclave told me her neighbors used to say: roughly translated, it means when the goyish world modernizes, so does the Jewish one. And, of course, when you crave such insularity, you run the danger of letting a desire for ideological consistency harden into a xenophobia that erodes some of the foundational missions of the faith, which include, for Jews, loving and welcoming the stranger, or serving as a light unto the nations.

I couldn't help but grimace at the reaction of a Colombian pastor who converted to Judaism and emigrated to Israel when he discovered his children were playing with the children of newly arrived Russian families ("most likely they are not Jewish at all," he balked, even though he himself hadn't been Jewish until recently). Or laugh, when I saw clips of Haredi revelers at a Jerusalem wedding belting out a tune that had been written specifically for

> **I stopped believing that any individual or group could so fully purify their environments that they would not have to grapple with the questions people everywhere are asking of themselves.**

the hit show *Shtisel*, about a Haredi family in Jerusalem – this, despite the fact that Haredim are said to never watch TV at all.

UNDERNEATH MY HEALTHY SKEPTICISM, I ultimately believe some amount of Jewish separatism is vital to our preservation. My family remained in Brooklyn for two more Halloweens after the swastika incident, although the second one basically didn't happen because of Covid. At first, I felt like the experience had taught me a valuable lesson about how to help my children understand what it meant to be a minority in America, and solidified for me that there were graceful ways to stand proudly but gently as a visible *ger v'toshav* in the world. But I eventually came to feel that being conspicuously peculiar, and maintaining a lifestyle that was largely foreign to our neighbors, was more heartache than it was worth. So we relocated to an area of the city that has a much higher concentration of observant Jews. We now live within walking distance of no fewer than five Orthodox synagogues, my son is always one of many children at the local playground wearing a kippah, and his playmates are not bugging him to go trick-or-treating come late October.

The decision to move to a more robust Jewish community wasn't simply a fleeing *from*; in a greater sense, it was really a running *toward*. Because so much of Jewish worship is communal, and happens over the natural course of our days – praying together, eating together, or being present for one another when babies are born and people pass away – living in areas with sparse Jewish populations deprived me of one of my religion's greatest paths to fulfillment.

I still have non-Jewish neighbors, and our friends here do vary in their levels of religious observance. There is a degree of cultural conformity that I'm unwilling to accept, for myself and for my children. And because I am

a convert – an actual *ger v'toshav*, an outsider both in the Jewish world and the wider one – I would be that much more conspicuous, and viewed much more suspiciously, in a shtetl, no matter how hard I tried to assimilate.

How separatist should a religious Jew be? How do you build fences without building fortresses? I thought of this during this past holiday of Sukkot, during which we eat in small huts outdoors, to remind us of the period the Jews spent wandering the desert post-Exodus. Like many things in Judaism, there are strict requirements for a sukkah: it must be at least three feet tall, have three walls, and the sky must be visible through the roof. Now that we have a backyard of our own, we were finally able to construct a sukkah for the first time. We fitted together the tall metal rods that comprised the "building," and then unrolled the bamboo sheets atop the scaffolding to make our roof. We were in a rush, as we often are, and so had to forgo the sometimes-elaborate decorations people put up, making do with the ivy spilling over from our garden into the interior as organic décor, and using only a few strips of plastic lattice instead of the tarps many use as walls. At first, I felt like ours looked almost pitifully unfinished.

But then one afternoon, I walked home from shul with my family, greeting the multiple Jewish passersby with a hearty *chag sameach* – happy holidays – all the while contemplating what it means to live apart but alongside the people on the sidewalk with whom I did not share a lifestyle. As I approached our house, I saw the sukkah in the distance, and realized that it was the answer to my question: a strong, sturdy little hut, designed to withstand the elements, distinct from the space around it, but wide open, as if to say to the strangers looking from outside, "Welcome. Come in." ❧

Eyvind Earle,
Reflections

Consider the Shiver

It was an easy road but stricken with glitter,
always horizon as a vision of home.
It was vital and virtual, drowsily actual, like a cloud on water.
Change, when it came, came so soft it seemed a seem.

Now time lies on the town like a town.
The streets are empty and the doors are shut.
God? Consider the shiver that goes through still water like a sound.
Who would we have to be to hear it?

CHRISTIAN WIMAN

EUGENE VODOLAZKIN

How Funerals Differ

Burying My Father

WHEN I WENT TO PARIS in mid-March 2016 for the Salon du Livre, I stayed at a hotel near the Place de la République. I was free that first evening, so I decided to take a walk. On my walks, I always give myself a destination, even if it's arbitrary: without that, movement loses meaning for me. This time I decided to go to Père Lachaise. The cemetery is beautiful and quite convincing as an endpoint (it is a cemetery, after all).

Père Lachaise is situated on a gently sloping hill, which I reached in forty minutes. It's a memorial cemetery, although initially it was not popular with the city's inhabitants (hard to believe now). Things got off the ground only when, for publicity purposes, to put it

Joe Smigielski,
Blue Mingus,
oil on canvas

before, in Ukraine, so far from Paris, I had buried my own father.

At the Père Lachaise gates I was met by two porters. I said hello; they didn't respond. Cemetery folk are stern. In no way did they encourage my presence, but they didn't keep me from going any farther, either. I walked on. Before turning down one of the cemetery streets (they have very real streets there), I looked back. The porters were silently watching me go. I understood that from there on I would be on my own; in all likelihood, there was no one else alive here.

My father. He was born in Nalchik and grew up in Baku; his ancestors were from the Volga and Stavropol. He wound up in Kyiv when he married my mother. They lived together for four years, gave birth to me, and then split up. I saw my father infrequently, even in my Kyiv childhood, and, once I'd moved to Saint Petersburg, very rarely. In a certain sense, his death made our visits more frequent; now all kinds of things would remind me of my father. A coat glimpsed in a crowd (he had the same kind), a similar vocal timbre over the radio.

At the cemetery I wondered: Is he responding to my thoughts of him *from there?* Can he tune in to my wavelength? Never having left the borders of the USSR, was he present now at Père Lachaise? I'm talking about a metaphysical presence, of course. There are no other options. Unlike Molière, there is no chance of my father's ashes being moved here. Not that there is really any need.

in modern terms, the ashes of La Fontaine and Molière were moved there. This made an impression on Paris's dead, and after that the cemetery started to grow by leaps and bounds. At various times, it has received the graves of Balzac, Proust, Wilde, Piaf, and even Ukrainian revolutionary Old Man Makhno, who got here God only knows how.

Actually, I'd been here before and hadn't come for their sakes. I liked the quiet of the place. The quiet of a city of the dead in the middle of a Paris seething with life. I may have been drawn here, too, because a few months

 MY FATHER IS BURIED in a village cemetery in the remote Ukrainian countryside. My father's second wife,

---

Eugene Vodolazkin's novel Laurus *won Russia's Big Book Award and the Yasnaya Polyana Book Award.* Plough *will be publishing Vodolazkin's novel* Brisbane *in April 2022 and his novel* A History of the Island *in 2023.*

Taisya, who comes from that village, is a good and considerate woman. She decided my father would rest more peacefully in the country. I think she's right, even though my father had never sought peace in his life.

During his four years in the navy, he would get up half an hour before reveille so as not to allow anyone to wake him. He always found legitimate opportunities to flout naval regulations. Upon his arrival in Kyiv, his daily routine did not get any simpler: morning and afternoon, the factory; then evening classes at the polytechnic institute; and at night unloading train cars because money was in drastically short supply. Each semester he would get a notice expelling him from the institute. He would take it to the dean's office and curtly and angrily demand reinstatement. He had no doubt that his anger was justified: they should try studying after a night at the freight station and a day at the factory. They always reinstated him. What else could they do?

Later, in exactly the same way, he prevented one of our relatives from being denied entry into regular high school after the eighth grade. My father didn't want him to go to a vocational school.

"But that's the same kind of school Korolev graduated from, you'll note . . ." the principal countered weakly.

"Well, if the boy were Korolev, I wouldn't object to the school," my father cut him off. "But he isn't Korolev."

I learned of my father's death one night, and the next day, without waiting for a telegram of confirmation, I flew to Kyiv. I flew via Minsk, forewarned that without that telegram complications might arise with the Ukrainian border guards. They didn't. The border guards asked the purpose of my visit and let me through without a murmur. I guess we're still one nation.

Early in the morning, Taisya, my stepbrother Sasha, and I picked up my father from the morgue. They put the casket in a van, a Gazelle, that had come from the village. We got into Sasha's car and drove ahead of the Gazelle. As we were leaving Kyiv, we stopped at a market to buy flowers; this took about ten minutes. When we got back, we found the Gazelle's driver in a state of bitter mirth: there are facial expressions common to crying and laughing. He pointed to the police car next to him. He'd parked illegally. I offered to talk to the police, but the driver just gestured in despair:

*"You think they're people? Animals."** *

The people he was talking about were writing a ticket – or rather the one in the front seat was writing, the other was standing, leaning against the car, smoking. I headed toward them anyway. Basically, I was on my way to pay. They saw me coming closer but didn't turn away. I said hello and then:

"I'm taking my father to be buried. Do we need to pay a fine?"

No pressure, no expression even, you might say. The one sitting stopped writing though. He released air noisily through fingers pressed to his lips. An unnaturally long "f." He wiped his forehead and leaned back in his seat.

"No, you don't."

How's that for you: *No, you don't.* Rather unexpected even. I shook the policeman's hand and got into my brother's car. The Gazelle's driver looked at me with respect. Cheerful music filtered out from his cab. Let my father listen; he liked music like that. When he was tight, he used to sing Soviet songs.

 THERE WAS MUSIC PLAYING at Père Lachaise, too. Not Soviet, naturally, but not bad, either: jazz, presumably. Drifting in from far off, it was barely audible:

* Throughout, italics indicate Ukrainian.

not even music so much as a beat being knocked out by a double bass. You don't get that effect with amplification. In disregard of the emotional state of any listeners, *live* music was playing at the cemetery. I moved slowly toward the sounds. Yes, jazz.

MY STEPBROTHER SASHA. He stepped on the gas, and I pictured my father in his casket bouncing over the potholes in the Gazelle behind us. Maybe even in time to the music. Sasha was in a hurry because we had to get to the village by a certain time. He spoke to someone on the phone occasionally and gave brief instructions in Ukrainian regarding the funeral. A downpour was followed by sunshine, which lit up shyly in the drops on the windshield. Then the downpour started back up. Without taking his eyes off the road, Sasha expressed the hope that the clouds would part because if there was going to be a downpour it would wash off our father's makeup. Yes, I agreed, that would be unpleasant. I'd forgotten they had applied makeup at the morgue.

Upon our arrival it became clear that our haste had been for nothing. There wasn't a trace of bustle in the village. People would walk up to the vehicles stopped by the church and then walk away, walk up again, and this time stay, come to a stillness, arms crossed at the chest (hands shoved in pockets, or stuck behind the lapel of a quilted jacket), sometimes scratching their cheeks and making an emery-board sound. They smoked.

Someone said we should go pick up Tonya, so Sasha and I drove to the next street for Tonya. After a brief wait, there appeared on the garden path an old woman bent ninety degrees at the waist. Leaning on two crutches, she moved slowly toward us. The synchronized movements of her arms and legs held something as athletic as it was exotic, something akin to beetles

racing. Though she was bent, Tonya's head was lifted, and her big eyes looked at us without blinking. We delivered her to the church.

Two supports for the casket and a wooden construction in the form of the letter п with several holes drilled in it floated slowly down the street. When all this was inside the church, my stepbrother and I and a few other men carried my father's casket in and set it on the supports. The church, which was gradually filling with people, was cold. A few people went

He stepped on the gas, and I pictured my father in his casket bouncing over the potholes in the Gazelle behind us. Maybe even in time to the music.

outside to warm up before the service started. The п-shaped construction was placed over the casket, and candles were inserted in the holes. It seemed to me that when they were lit it got warmer. The sight of fire, no matter how small, always makes it warmer. More joyful, too, perhaps. Surrounded by dozens of agitated flames, my father no longer looked so doleful.

A woman was binding his feet and was about to bind his hands but noticed that only his left arm was resting on his chest. For some reason, his right was extended alongside his body. The woman froze with an astonished face. She didn't understand how to bind the hands in this instance. I didn't either, nor did I understand why this had to be done before the service.

Joe Smigielski,
Blue Cat Crew,
oil on canvas, 2016

Evidently, it had its own hidden meaning.

"It won't bend," the woman said.

Amid the general silence, Tonya hobbled toward the casket.

"I'll bend it."

She leaned both her crutches against the casket and picked up my father's arm. I tensed inwardly, but she pressed his right hand to his left without special effort. Indeed, it was a good thing we'd brought Tonya. Now nothing prevented the woman with the rope from binding my father's hands.

I raised my eyes and saw the priest, who had just entered. He was standing at the head of the casket, thoughtfully observing the binding. The service was held with the same calm dignity with which everything in this village was done, evidently.

"Have you bound God's servant German?" the priest asked when the women had finished.

"Yes, we have, father."

I saw they'd bound him.

"Well, then, go with God."

A few instructions were given in that divine language which my father, in all the years he lived in Kyiv, never did learn. A few minutes later, an old Zhiguli with a trailer drove up to the church doors, and the open casket was placed on the trailer, which was nearly as imposing as a gun carriage.

The procession started moving. Up ahead was a man with a cross, a little behind him two men with gonfalons, behind them the priest and chorus, then the Zhiguli with my father on the trailer, behind the trailer Taisya, Sasha, and I, and behind us Tonya (with a mongrel to either side), and then the entire village. The Zhiguli drove slowly, but the unpaved road was bumpy. My father's arms (especially the right one Tonya had bent) started lifting up. His elbows were still resting on his stomach, but now his hands were hovering in the air.

Lying in his casket, my father looked like he was talking to heaven. His arms were swaying, which lent the conversation a peaceful and even casual look.

It was about half a kilometer to the cemetery. Every hundred meters, the procession would halt and the priest, accompanied by the singers, would recite prayers for the repose of the dead. Compared with our drive, our time at the cemetery felt short. When the first clods of earth struck my father's casket, I was shocked at how loud they were. They were like a drum and not at all in accordance with the funeral's quiet. After the grave was filled in, everyone headed for the funeral repast at the café directly opposite the ceremony. I was about to follow them, but someone stopped me:

"The relatives have their own path."

"Path" in Ukrainian is feminine. I don't know what that implies, if anything. They showed me the way only relatives of the deceased were supposed to go. I was joined by Taisya and Sasha, and fifteen minutes later we were at the café. After the prayer read by the priest, silence reigned. That is, from time to time you'd hear a quiet murmur, or utensils clattering, but there were no general conversations, to say nothing of toasts. The prayers were the toasts.

A JAZZ BAND WAS PLAYING at Père Lachaise. When I reached the music's sounds, I observed the casket floating slowly through the crematorium doors to the blues. I hadn't known there was a crematorium at this cemetery, but most of all, I never would have thought it was active. That right here, you could lie down without further ado, or at worst have your ashes scattered next to Sarah Bernhardt, Beaumarchais, or, say, Chopin. It turns out, you could – and to remarkable music as well.

It was truly professional playing, not some cemetery band. It wasn't a cemetery repertoire either. They understood each other at the slightest hint, nodded to each other and made faces – the way jazz musicians are supposed to. They improvised. The rays of the setting sun lent them a redness. Especially a woman in a provocatively scarlet coat, who positively blazed. She wasn't playing anything, she was just standing there next to the musicians, tapping her foot. Her face was decorated with a clown nose – also red, held on by an elastic strap.

Some were going into the crematorium building, others coming out. It was like a party at the moment the general gaiety has died down and each prefers to find his own spot. Hesitant, I stopped at the door, but someone (such a hospitable institution) opened it and asked:

"Excuse me, are you coming in?"

"Yes. Of course."

Just from my laconic speech he realized immediately I wasn't French. He smiled, as if to say, what does a foreigner need a crematorium for? And indeed, what did I? Although I knew the answer, of course. I'd needed a toilet for a while, the usual cemetery story, because at cemeteries it's cool and windy.

I found the restroom by following the signs. Sitting outside it on a chair was a good-looking attendant (in Paris they're called "Madame Pipi"), and for some reason I immediately realized she was one of us. The way a customs officer unerringly susses out a smuggler, someone who has lived abroad for a long time (as I had) easily recognizes his compatriots. I addressed her in Russian. She replied with a slightly provincial accent. Taking advantage of this unexpected encounter, she told me how lots of people miss when they pee – decent people to look at them, but in fact . . .

"Comes with the job," I joked.

She gave me a dubious look.

Little by little, everyone gathered in the open area in front of the crematorium. The band sparkled with magical improvisation. I went up to someone standing at the edge and asked:

"Excuse me, what is this?"

"A funeral."

"An unusual one."

If I can resort to an oxymoron, I'd say a cemetery should be alive. That is, while being memorial, it should not forget its primordial calling.

He nodded. I wanted to asked something else but couldn't bring myself to. Actually, I didn't understand what exactly there was to ask.

The woman with the clown nose gathered everyone in a circle and invited them to dance. The band switched to folk tunes. At least they felt folk to me because they were simple and beautiful. And people were dancing folk-style to them, with toe-tapping and clapping. I wanted to dance, too, but I realized that would be a bit much for a guest of the capital.

"Who is this woman?" I did find a question for my interlocutor.

"The widow. Her husband was a jazz musician."

When the widow walked past us, I noticed that her eyes were wet with tears.

"But why did she put on the nose?"

He squeezed his own nose between two fingers and said nasally:

"She's expressing her contempt for death."

Is that so. I stood there a little longer and then moved toward the exit. I wasn't leaving the cemetery yet, I just decided to stroll closer to the exit. For some reason it occurred to me how easy it would be for people strolling in the far corners to get locked in for the night. On the road I saw another funeral procession. This time the casket was being carried to an open grave, not the crematorium. That means you don't have to be in the form of ashes to be buried in Père Lachaise. Well, that's good. If I can resort to an oxymoron, I'd say a cemetery should be alive. That is, while being memorial, it should not forget its primordial calling. Outsiders weren't being let into the second funeral. Cemetery employees stood on the path, cutting off any gawkers. Probably so as not to attract attention, funerals here are scheduled for the evening.

At the gate I ran into the jazz musicians. Even as they were walking out, they kept on playing. Evidently they were on their way to the nearest bistro to commemorate the deceased. So as not to give the impression that I'd set my sights on joining them, I crossed to the other side of the street. My interlocutor recognized me and, shouting over the band, reminded me: "Contempt for death!" He raised his two clasped hands. I repeated the gesture, and we stood there like that for a few seconds. Total solidarity. I recalled my father's raised arms – also an expression of contempt for death. Perhaps not as vivid as in Paris (different funerals, to say the least), but also quite definite. He'd just died and he was already looking over. Over its head. Death's.

This essay was originally published in Russian in Esquire *(Russia Edition) on August 22, 2016. Translated by Marian Schwartz.*

One Star above All Stars

Ignatius of Antioch

Ignatius, the patriarch of Antioch, is traditionally considered to have been a disciple of John the Apostle. This reading is taken from his Letter to the Ephesians, *written on his way to martyrdom in Rome, ca. AD 108.*

OUR GOD, JESUS the Christ, was conceived by Mary according to God's plan, both from the seed of David and of the Holy Spirit. He was born and was baptized in order that by his suffering he might cleanse the water. >>

NOW THE VIRGINITY of Mary and her giving birth were hidden from the ruler of this age, as was also the death of the Lord – three mysteries to be loudly proclaimed, yet which were accomplished in the silence of God.

How, then, were they revealed to the ages?

About the artist:
John August Swanson
(1938–2021)

John August Swanson, who died in September 2021, once said his art is about bringing stories to life, infusing the world with a vision of the holy, and discovering the divine in the everyday. His art reflects the gift of story-telling he inherited from his Mexican mother and his Swedish father. John's narrative art explores the cultural roots of our human experience and the religious stories that are the founda-tion of the Christian faith. The three Advent serigraphs in this piece are: *Shepherds* (1985), *Nativity* (1988), and *Epiphany* (1988).

A STAR SHONE FORTH

in heaven brighter than all the stars; its light was indescribable and its strangeness caused amazement. All the rest of the constellations, together with the sun and moon, formed a chorus around the star, yet the star itself far outshone them all, and there was perplexity about the origin of this strange phenomenon, which was so unlike the others.

Consequently all magic and every kind of spell were dissolved, the ignorance so characteristic of wickedness vanished, and the ancient kingdom was abolished when God appeared in human form to bring the newness of eternal life; and what had been prepared by God began to take effect. As a result, all things were thrown into ferment, because the abolition of death was being carried out. ➤

Trans. Michael W. Holmes, *The Apostolic Fathers* (Baker Academic, 2007). Used by permission.

PLOUGH BOOKLIST

New Releases

Breaking Ground: Charting Our Future in a Pandemic Year

Mark Noll, N. T. Wright, Gracy Olmstead, Jennifer Frey, Michael Wear, Danté Stewart, Marilynne Robinson, Christine Emba, Tara Isabella Burton, Phil Christman, Jeffrey Bilbro, L. M. Sacasas, Oliver O'Donovan, and more

Edited by Anne Snyder and Susannah Black

As a pandemic and racial reckoning exposed society's faults, Christian thinkers were laying the groundwork for a better future. In the spring of 2020, *Comment* magazine, along with *Plough* and others, created a publishing project to tap the resources of a Christian humanist tradition to respond collaboratively and imaginatively to these crises. The web commons that resulted – *Breaking Ground* – became a one-of-a-kind space to probe society's assumptions and imagine what a better future might require.

This volume, written in real time during a year that revealed the depths of our society's fissures, provides a wealth of reflections and proposals on what should come after. It is an anthology of different lenses of faith seeking to understand how best we can serve the broader society and renew our civilization.

John Milbank, University of Nottingham: If you despair of the future, the writers represented here offer real prophetic hope.

Hardcover, 468 pages, ~~$35.00~~ **$21.00 with subscriber discount**

Following the Call: Living the Sermon on the Mount Together

Eberhard Arnold, Augustine, Wendell Berry, Dietrich Bonhoeffer, Dorothy Day, Meister Eckhart, Timothy Keller, Søren Kierkegaard, Martin Luther King Jr., C. S. Lewis, Richard Rohr, Dorothy L. Sayers, Rabindranath Tagore, Barbara Brown Taylor, Mother Teresa, Leo Tolstoy, N. T. Wright, and ninety-four others

Edited by Charles E. Moore

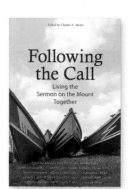

Jesus' most famous teaching, the Sermon on the Mount, possesses an irresistible quality. Who hasn't felt stirred and unsettled after reading these words, which get to the root of the human condition? This anthology is designed to be read together with others, to inspire communities of faith to discuss what it might look like to put these radical teachings into practice today.

Russell Moore, *Christianity Today*: This book will prompt you to surprise, to delight, to melancholy, to argument, and, at every turn, will lead you back to Jesus.

Shane Claiborne, author, *The Irresistible Revolution*: There are no words more important than the Sermon on the Mount. And I can think of no better cloud of witnesses to reflect on those words than the people in this book.

Softcover, 396 pages, ~~$18.00~~ **$10.80 with subscriber discount**

Books That Honor Vulnerability

Perfectly Human: Nine Months with Cerian
Sarah C. Williams

Happily married and teaching at Oxford, Sarah C. Williams had credentials, success, and knowledge. It would take someone with none of these things to teach her what matters in life. This extraordinary memoir begins with the welcome news of a new member of the Williams family. Sarah's husband, Paul, and their two young daughters share her excitement. But the happiness is short-lived, as a hospital scan reveals skeletal dysplasia. The doctor says birth will be fatal. To the surprise of medical staff and professional colleagues, Sarah and Paul decide to carry the baby to term. Here is Sarah's candid and heart-stretching account of the intimate journey towards her daughter's birthday. (Read her article on page 22.)

Christianity Today: A profoundly moving and wise book. . . . Williams shifts seamlessly between intimate reflections on love in the midst of tragic loss and incisive commentary on the social structures that framed her experience.

Softcover, 160 pages, ~~$16.00~~ **$9.60 with subscriber discount**

If My Moon Was Your Sun
Andreas Steinhöfel
Illustrations by Nele Palmtag

Did you hear the story about Max, the boy who kidnapped his grandfather from a nursing home?

A touching story about dementia and the special relationship between grandparents and grandchildren, with full-color illustrations and an audiobook featuring twelve classical pieces for children by Georges Bizet and Sergei Prokofiev.

School Library Journal: With its loving portrayal of aging, caring for the elderly, and the keen nature of kids' sensibilities, this is a must-purchase for all libraries serving children.

Hardcover, 80 pages, ~~$19.00~~ **$11.40 with subscriber discount**

The Prince Who Was Just Himself
Silke Schnee
Illustrated by Heike Sistig

The royal couple is looking forward to their third child. "He looks a little different," muses the king at Prince Noah's arrival. "He is not like the others," agrees the queen. Soon they notice what a very special person he is, even though he can't do everything his brothers can. When the youngest prince disarms the cruel knight Scarface, the nation's most dreaded enemy, with an act of compassion, everyone finally realizes how good it is that each person is unique. This delightfully illustrated fairy tale instills appreciation for children with Down syndrome and other developmental challenges, making it a valuable aid for teaching tolerance in the home or classroom.

Hardcover, 32 pages, ~~$16.00~~ **$9.60 with subscriber discount**

Christmas Gifts

Home for Christmas: Stories for Young and Old

Pearl Buck, Rebecca Caudill, Ruth Sawyer, Elizabeth Goudge, Selma Lagerlöf, Henry van Dyke, and others

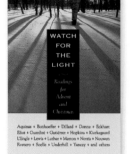

They are some of the warmest childhood memories, those unhurried evenings around the fireplace, Christmas tree, or dinner table, when there was time for a story . . . Now, with this collection, you can keep the storytelling tradition alive in your family, and pass it on to your children or grandchildren.

Home for Christmas includes twenty time-honored tales. Several are by world-famous authors; others are little-known treasures translated from other languages. Selected for their literary quality and spiritual integrity, they will resonate with readers of all ages, year after year. *Now in a deluxe hardcover gift edition.*

Jim Trelease, author, *The Read-Aloud Handbook*: If you're giving one book for Christmas, make it this one.

Hardcover, 339 pages, ~~$22.00~~ **$13.20 with subscriber discount**

Watch for the Light: Readings for Advent and Christmas

Dorothy Day, C. S. Lewis, Oscar Romero, Philip Yancey, Dietrich Bonhoeffer, Alfred Delp, Søren Kierkegaard, Annie Dillard, Kathleen Norris, and others

Though Christians the world over make yearly preparations for Lent, there's a conspicuous lack of good books for that other great spiritual season: Advent. Ecumenical in scope, these fifty devotions invite the reader to contemplate the great themes of Christmas and the significance that the coming of Jesus has for each of us – not only during Advent, but every day.

***Publishers Weekly*:** These are not frivolous, feel-good Advent readings; they are deep, sometimes jarring reflections, many with a strong orientation toward social justice. . . . This collection, born of obvious passion and graced with superb writing, is a welcome – even necessary – addition.

Hardcover, 344 pages, ~~$24.00~~ **$14.40 with subscriber discount**

Evening Prayers: For Every Day of the Year

Christoph Friedrich Blumhardt

We want to turn to God at the end of each day, but often don't find the words to express our deepest feelings and longing. This collection of prayers is one of the few daily devotionals especially intended for use in the evening. Blumhardt's words bespeak a certainty in God's nearness. The peace that flows from them comes from an unshakeable conviction that God's kingdom is indeed on the way. In stormy and challenging times like our own, most of us need this reassurance frequently, if not daily.

Luci Shaw, author, *Water My Soul*: This book of prayers is a treasure, a precious pearl. May others discover its riches, as I have.

Karl Barth: Blumhardt's message is a most spontaneous and penetrating word of God, and it speaks right into the need of the world.

Hardcover, 408 pages, ~~$20.00~~ **$12.00 with subscriber discount**

Flannery O'Connor

As a writer with a disability, the beloved Southern novelist showed the beauty of a costly life.

SUSANNAH BLACK

"**G**RACE CHANGES US and the change is painful," wrote Flannery to Cecil Dawkins in 1958. This is why "human nature vigorously resists grace."

Opposite: Katherine Sandoz, Flannery O'Connor in Gucci, 2016

Flannery O'Connor knew about pain. Diagnosed with lupus at twenty-five, she spent most of the rest of her life living with her mother at Andalusia, the family farm near Milledgeville, Georgia. As the lupus and the side effects of its treatment progressively weakened her, she wrote. The steroids that treated her softened her bones; she had to use crutches to walk. Every day, she wrote, she attended Mass, she read and rested in the afternoon. Between her return to Georgia and her death, she completed two novels, more than two dozen short stories, and numerous essays, and kept up a lively correspondence close to home and much farther afield.

She died August 3, 1964, seven years after she had been told she wouldn't live long. She was buried in Milledgeville, age thirty-nine.

Though she'd left Georgia at twenty to attend the Iowa Writers' Workshop, and spent time writing at Yaddo in New York and at a friend's home in Connecticut, she was always very much a Southern writer. "Anything that comes out of the South is going to be called grotesque by the northern reader," she once said tartly, "unless it is grotesque, in which case it is going to be called realistic."

Flannery O'Connor is one of the most evocative writers of the gospel in fiction who has ever lived. "The stories," she wrote, "are hard but they are hard because there is nothing harder or less sentimental than Christian realism. . . . When I see these stories described as horror stories I am always amused because the reviewer always has hold of the wrong horror."

Her stories return repeatedly to themes of pain, sickness, and physical disability; violence, social cruelty, and personal sin are their analogues. Such stories as "Everything That Rises Must Converge," "Good Country People," and "Greenleaf" show characters whose moral growth, when it comes, comes in and through pain: when, in the middle of weakness and suffering, the wretchedness of humanity is touched by grace: transfigured.

Flannery's preoccupation with both the morally grotesque and the physically disabled is related to her preoccupation with the fall of man. She suggested as much in an essay: "When you have to assume that [your audience is not Christian], then you have to make your vision apparent by shock – to the hard of hearing you shout, and for the almost-blind you draw large and startling figures." Her audience assumed, in its midcentury optimism, that everything was OK. But everything is not OK. There is something wrong with

(continued on p. 111)

Susannah Black is a Plough *senior editor.*

(continued from p. 112)

humanity. There is something unnatural in nature. Lucynell is deaf and an innocent; Mr. Shiftlet has lost half an arm and is a heartless manipulator. Hulda's artificial leg, even her smug philosophical atheism, are less a disability than the Bible salesman's empty-souled hypocritical cruelty.

It's not that the physical disability of her characters reflects moral grotesquerie; the physical is an analogue for the moral. The same wreck that wrecks the bodies wrecks the souls of men, and the society they're living in. Flannery herself is an example of this. Though she had a keen eye for the viciousness of racism in her society, she at times participated in it, as recent scholars have suggested.

Flannery, I believe, would have had no trouble accepting that the not-OK-ness of humanity extended to herself as well. After all, this recognition lies at the heart of Christianity. In that letter to Cecil Dawkins, Flannery reminded her that "the church is founded on Peter who denied Christ three times and couldn't walk on water by himself."

Peter's faithless denial of Christ and his faltering as he walked to his Lord across the sea don't end the story, because grace breaks in. There's not always justice in O'Connor's stories, or transformation, or redemption. But they hover around the edges of the text, shimmering behind it, glimpsed out of the corner of the eye.

These glimpses hint that, for O'Connor, disability may well be a metaphor or counterpoint to sin, but that it is not the end of the story. For her, even the grotesque – the sign of humanity's not-OK-ness – also bears a positive meaning. As the critic Timothy Basselin has contended, the grotesque is, for O'Connor, beauty too. It gestures towards the beauty of our own limitedness, our dependence, the beauty of a costly life.

Flannery O'Connor, 1962

Famously, Flannery took up raising peacocks after she returned to Milledgeville, eventually raising more than two hundred. The tail of the peacock is the classic example of what has been called the "handicap principle" in evolutionary biology. Proposed in 1975 by the Israeli biologists Amotz and Avishag Zahavi, this hypothesis seeks to explain such extravagant and seemingly useless evolutionary developments as the peacock's tail. It's costly for a male peacock to grow and then cart around such a tail. It takes a great deal of extra energy to grow it, and once it's grown, it makes it harder for him to fly. But this costliness is, Zahavi hypothesized, a pledge of honesty. "I'm not just pretending to have resources of strength," the peacock says. "If I didn't have them I couldn't afford this extravagant thing." It signals that the one bearing the handicap is, to precisely the degree of the disadvantage, strong.

The riches that Flannery had came from the treasurehouse of Christ and his church. They enabled her to bear her disability with grace, fruitfulness, and wit – and grotesque, extravagant beauty. ➤